D0397884

MAYA
SCRIPT

MARIA LONGHENA

MAYA
SCRIPT

A CIVILIZATION AND ITS WRITING

Translated from the Italian by
ROSANNA M. GIAMMANCO FRONGIA

ABBEVILLE PRESS   PUBLISHERS
New York   London   Paris

Front and back covers: *Details from a stucco panel in relief on the rear wall of the sanctuary, in the Temple of the Sun, Palenque*

English Language Edition
Translator: Rosanna M. Giammanco Frongia
Editor: Mary Christian
Cover Designer: Paula Winicur

First published in the United States of America in 2000 by Abbeville Press, 22 Cortlandt Street, New York, NY 10007

The text of this book was set in Meno. Printed and bound in Spain by Artes Graficas Toledo, S.A.
D.L. TO: 1291 - 2000

First edition
10 9 8 7 6 5 4 3 2 1

Library of Congress Cataloging-in-Publication Data

Longhena, María.
    Mayan script : a civilization revealed through the signs / María Longhena ; translated by Rosanna M. Giammanco Frongia.
        p. cm.
    Includes bibliographical references and index.
    ISBN 0-7892-0653-6 (alk. paper)
    1. Mayan languages—Writing. 2. Inscriptions, Mayan. 3. Maya—Social life and customs. I. Title.

F1435.3.W75 L65 2000
972.81'016—dc21   00-022495

CONTENTS

KEY TO THE NOTES

Below are a few helpful comments about the layout of the pages in the glyph chapters.

The page title is the term expressed by the glyph. In some cases, it is a subject strictly related to the glyph.

BALL GAME

The two glyphs on the left refer respectively to the "ball game" and the "ball player." It was not a sport, rather a ritual practice common to all of Mesoamerica.

The glyph, taken from epigraphic inscriptions or codices, may be an ideographic sign, a phonetic sign, or a mixed sign. Two glyphs next to each other can express a single concept or two interrelated concepts.

The caption next to the glyph is a short, introductory description of the glyph.

In all of Mesoamerica, playing ball was not a sport, but a true ritual. A spheristerion, the court where the games were held, was found even at the Olmec site of La Venta, evidence that this ancient practice originated with the Olmec. Proof of this practice was also found in other important centers such as El Tajín and Monte Albán, as well as in all the Maya and Aztec regions. There were different kinds of ball courts: those used by the Maya had two goal rings set into opposite walls, corresponding to midfield.

The game was played by the nobility to resolve territorial claims or marriages, and to hold tournaments. People would bet on the winner. Often, the captain of the losing team

This vase painting, probably from Calakmul, shows two ball players wearing game outfits. Dallas Museum of Art.

The illustration of the glyph is often drawn from an archaeological find and complements the text, highlighting interesting aspects of Maya life.

When the glyph's concept also appears in another pre-Columbian civilization, a comparative text is added, enclosed in a box and sometimes complemented by a representative illustration from that civilization.

The Aztec Ball Game

The ball game, called pelota by the Spaniards, was played in all major Mesoamerican civilizations. This illustration from the Codex Borbonicus shows a game court (also called the spheristerion) in the shape of the letter I, typical of Aztec culture. Unlike earlier times, at the time of Moctezuma the game had acquired a different meaning and had become a sort of game of chance, on whose outcome bets were placed, even of the most precious property.

was sacrificed by decapitation; this is what chroniclers reported and this is what can be inferred by analyzing Postclassic paintings. The rules of the game were as follows: two teams of players threw a solid rubber ball into the enemy camp, sometimes throwing it inside a stone ring placed high on the wall. Players could not use hands or feet to touch the ball. The players protected their knees and heads with stiff, heavily padded deer-leather gear, as may be observed from stone copies made by Maya sculptors.

Apparently, this cruel ritual was linked to sun worship, the ball representing the sun. The players were expected never to let the ball fall to the ground, so that sometimes these games lasted several days. The movement of the sun, and the blood that was shed, fertilized the earth and promoted a bountiful harvest.

MEN 155

The text analyzes the concept contained in the glyph, its innermost meaning, and its origin and place in Maya culture.

This page helps the reader to understand the central section of this work, the pages that interpret the glyphs.

Each page begins with a drawing and a brief description of the glyph, where we present the content it expresses, in cases where the meaning of the glyph has been clearly established. Readers wishing to learn more about the technical aspects of deciphering these symbols will find valuable suggestions for further reading at the back of this book.

The glyph chapters are divided by subject. The first chapter covers life at court, looking at the leading cities where Maya culture flourished, the high-ranking dignitaries who shaped the life of the cities, and some unusual aspects of life at court, such as civil or religious ceremonies. The chapter devoted to symbols includes the cardinal points that are fundamental in Maya cosmogony and the numbers from one to twenty. The next chapter covers the major deities in the Maya religious pantheon. In the chapter devoted to the months of the Maya solar calendar, rather than following a simple chronological order, we preferred a sequence based on the nature of each period's ritual. The last two chapters discuss the glyphs that refer to celestial bodies and to nature and its sacredness.

FOREWORD

We owe the first reports about pre-Columbian American civilizations to the Spanish chroniclers at the time of the conquest. Their reports uniformly agreed in denying that the Maya possessed a writing system, although they noted that painted books had been found in Mexico. We can explain this apparent contradiction by recalling that the Western mentality of the time accepted as "writing" only those systems consisting of letters from an alphabet, and usually classified that as the goal of other, more primitive writing systems that were considered inferior.

From an anthropological point of view, the difference between alphabet writing and pictographic, ideographic, and philographic writings—or any combinations of these—consists in the number of possible expressions and the precision of meaning it allows.

I believe the publishers made an excellent choice in dedicating a book to Maya writing as an introduction to the concept of anthropological writing in the ancient Americas. The Maya culture is one of the more meaningful in this context, and offers excellent examples of the paths American man followed to reach civilization, which differ from those of the Old World.

If we were to apply to the Maya the strict parameters used to measure cultural development in the Old World, they would be classified as a stone-age civilization, since all their cutting tools were made of such stones as flint and obsidian. When, in the waning centuries of their civilization, the Maya discovered copper, bronze, and gold, they used these metals merely as materials for decoration.

Yet the Maya built cities whose palaces and monuments continue to amaze us today. They were also great mathematicians and astronomers, having discovered positional mathematics and the meaning of zero at least two centuries before European man. As early as the seventh century A.D. they had calculated the solar year to be 365.2420 days, with a truly minuscule difference from the calculation adopted in the West since 1582, which is 365.2423 days.

We should note that all this lively concern with astronomy and mathematics was due to the Maya obsession—which they shared with all the peoples of Mesoamerica—with the passing of time.

For these peoples, time was very concrete, somehow coinciding with the movement of the sun. They were convinced that time was cyclical, to the point that the Maya believed that by studying past astronomical and astrological events they could predict future ones. They also believed that each god personified itself in the sky in a celestial body, and on earth in an animal.

In order to mark everyday life and all kinds of festivals and events, two calendars were used concurrently, and their courses progressed in a parallel manner. The first, the solar calendar, consisted of 360 plus 5 days; the second, the ritual calendar, was composed of 260 days. This meant that the two calendars returned to the same point of departure only at fifty-two-year intervals; at that point, a calendar round was completed. Furthermore, the Maya believed that the time/sun was carried, as a witness, by a sort of gigantic bearer consisting of the deities who were in charge of the specific days of both the solar and the ritual calendars. Day after day, the calendrical gods were charged with keeping time alive, carrying it from one deity to the other, while on earth the astronomers and astrologers followed the heavenly obstacles the bearers might encounter and tried to aid them with prayers, offerings, and sacrifices.

Since all of the divine bearers met every fifty-two years—at the end of each calendrical cycle—to all simultaneously change their guards of the time/sun witness, Mesoamericans awaited anxiously this particular moment. For if one of the gods would carelessly let the time/sun witness fall, the end of the world would ensue (since no other god could take the careless god's place and catch the time/sun, as they were all similarly engaged). We should note here that both the Aztec and the Maya peoples believed the end of the world had taken place several times before, and they were living in the fifth creation.

However, the Maya were able to avert the impending danger by studying the calendrical cycles of other planets, whose divine bearers would continue to carry the precious time/sun witness even if the fifty-two-year cycle should end, as they feared.

According to this highly complex system, which the Maya called the "Long Count," the fifth creation in which they believed they were living had begun in 3113 B.C. and would end in A.D. 2012. If we compare this system to our calendar, the Long Count permits us to assign an exact date to the Maya artifacts and monuments.

With the exception of the writing system that we are analyzing in this book, I think no other form of writing could have served Mesoamerican culture, for these peoples did not use writing to communicate with other men, but to link their rulers to the gods, to the sacredness of nature, and to the cosmos. The link was provided by glyphs, which were written in a rich and varied style and represented the subjects they addressed. Although glyphs were also used to express words that had no specific religious meaning, the glyphs nonetheless expressed a sacred nature they were endowed with. Whether written with conceptual or syllabic meanings, as key words or as phonetic signs, these symbols were a link to the sanctity of nature, the cosmos, and the gods.

This would not have been possible with words written using the abstract letters of any alphabet, since letters cannot individually express sacred meaning. Thus Maya writing had as an additional meaning—or perhaps as an essential element—this intimate link to the divine.

LAURA LAURENCICH MINELLI
Department of Paleography and Medieval Studies
University of Bologna

IN SEARCH OF A PEOPLE

When the European conquistadors landed on Mexican soil, the Maya cities had long since fallen into a state of decline and abandonment. Vegetation had overgrown the ancient palaces, pyramids, and steles, partially hiding the traces of what had been a great, mysterious civilization. In the following centuries, missionaries and explorers set out to unveil this mystery by attempting to decipher ancient Maya writing.

DISCOVERING THE WORLD OF THE MAYA

Today's traveler who visits the Maya archaeological sites scattered in the tropical forests of Yucatán and Guatemala or in Honduras, Belize, and El Salvador, is struck by the imposing, refined quality of the ancient stone structures one can glimpse in the midst of the dense vegetation. These monuments were built by a civilization that probably reached a higher cultural level than all the others that flourished in pre-Columbian America did, even developing a complex writing system.

In 1521, when the Spanish captain Hernán Cortés subdued the powerful Aztec kingdom, the Aztecs were at the apex of their splendor under Emperor Moctezuma II. Elsewhere, however, the Spanish conquistadors had discovered, several years earlier, the ruins of a mysterious civilization, in an almost complete state of decay, that was later called "Maya." Before going on to describe the Maya people's singular artistic and intellectual qualities, which are still somewhat of a puzzle to researchers, it is interesting to recall how the first Europeans met the surviving Indians of this most ancient culture.

In 1517 conquistador Hernández de Córdoba, after enslaving most of the natives on the islands of Cuba and Hispaniola (the latter is currently divided into Haiti and the Dominican Republic), organized an expedition to other sites in search of new slaves and, especially, gold. Moving west, he landed on an island near the northeastern Yucatán coast.

For the first time, the Spaniards noticed with surprise the existence of stone buildings, much more prestigious than the Indian huts they had seen until then. Inside those structures, which were probably temples, they found female idols and gold jewelry: for this reason, they called the island Isla Mujeres, "the women's island."

This episode may have been the first in which the Europeans encountered traces of the ancient world of the Maya. Later, Córdoba, who was excited about the discovery, set sail for Yucatán and landed near the city of Champotón, where for the first time the Spaniards encountered Maya people. Although frightened by the firearms that were unknown to them, the natives killed many of the invaders; Córdoba himself died from serious wounds suffered in

Below: *The conquistadors being sighted by natives as they land in Mexico.*

Above: *One of the imposing Copán steles depicting a city king from the Classic period. It was discovered by early explorers who first penetrated into the tropical forest looking for remains of a mysterious lost civilization.*
Opposite, above: *A drawing by Frederick Catherwood of two natives sitting before Chichén Itzá's Mayan ruins.*

the attack. In subsequent expeditions led by Juan de Grijalva in 1518, Hernán Cortés in 1525, and Francisco de Montejo in 1527, the Spaniards again attempted to conquer the Maya. They gradually came upon a large number of monumental ruins scattered in the jungle and partially buried under tropical vegetation, and understood that this was an ancient civilization of great interest.

The definitive conquest of the Mayan territories took place in 1542 under Spanish captain Francisco de Montejo the younger, who overcame all resistance among the native population and founded Mérida, the new capital of the province of Yucatán, on the ruins of the ancient city of Tihoo. At the time, groups of Franciscan friars had already been dispatched from Spain to approach the subjected indigenous populations and convert them. Their leading figure was Bishop Diego de Landa, whose fame rests on his tragic work of destruction, but also on his valuable written testimony, which described in great detail what was then, essentially, the last bulwark of the ancient Yucatán civilization.

DIEGO DE LANDA

Anxious to root out all forms of idolatry in the worship, rituals, and artifacts of the natives and to convert all of them to Christianity,

A Colonial-era miniature depicting an Aztec motif: a human sacrifice that required a bird-masked priest to pull out the victim's heart.

one year after the start of his mandate, in July 1562, de Landa organized an extensive campaign of destruction in the Maya city of Maní. After punishing with torture several Indian governors who were accused of continuing to practice idolatry as their ancestors had done, de Landa ordered the destruction in a gigantic bonfire of thousands of idols, dozens of steles and altars, hundreds of pottery vases, and about thirty manuscript rolls. This is how the bishop described the event: "We found many books written in their alphabet, whose contents were nothing but lies and diabolical superstition, and we burned them all, causing them much grief."

With this implacable destruction, Diego de Landa caused the loss of precious materials and burned a priceless written heritage: the many manuscripts he threw into the fire would have enabled posterity to more fully comprehend the thought and traditions of the Maya. Only four of these manuscripts survive—they will be discussed later in the book—

but they do not suffice to fill the enormous void this destruction left in our knowledge of the Maya people.

However, to defend himself from the accusation of engaging in overzealous repression, this Franciscan provincial began to take an intense interest in the Yucatán populations. He studied their customs, ways of thinking, aspects of their everyday lives, and even their art. He collected all his observations in his book *Relación de las cosas de Yucatán* (Account of the Things of Yucatán). His work is still the main source of information on the life and thought of the Maya at the time of the conquest, descendants of the Maya who had reached the apex of their civilization many centuries earlier.

The book's accounts of the various religious festivals are particularly interesting, as are the descriptions of the temples and other monumental buildings of numerous centers, including Chichén Itzá, Tihoo, and Izamal. Although

he did not know the history of the Maya people, de Landa concluded that whoever had built such grandiose works had reached an extremely advanced cultural level. He called the Maya "a civilized people," not "savages." The bishop-scholar also took an interest in the strange inscriptions he found engraved on what might be described as stone altars, especially steles that, according to the natives, their ancestors customarily erected every twenty years.

Unfortunately, Diego de Landa's book was forgotten after his death. It was published only in 1861, when the French abbot Brasseur de Bourbourg casually came upon it in Madrid and had it published in a bilingual version. Thus, apart from being an exceptional historical document, de Landa's book may be seen as the first step in the lengthy process undertaken by clerics, explorers, and scientists to study and learn the language of the Maya.

After de Landa's death, the Yucatán territo-

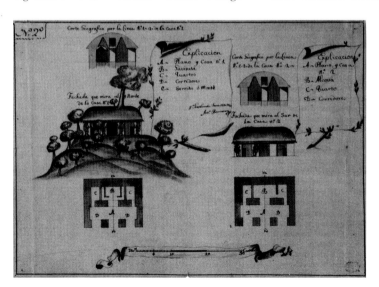

Above: *An eighteenth-century Palenque relief. According to Waldeck, the Maya king is shown in a style similar to that of Near Eastern rulers.* **Left:** *A seventeenth-century sketch of Palenque's Temple of the Sun and Temple of the Foliated Cross.* **Opposite, above:** *An early photograph of a Maya site, showing Quiriguá's Stele E, thirty-six feet (12 m) high.*

ries and the fascinating Maya ruins were abandoned and the early information that had been gathered about the Maya civilization was forgotten. When, in 1747, Father Solis was dispatched as a missionary to the city of Santo Domingo de Palenque, Mexico, he immediately came upon the spectacular remains of an ancient city that had long before fallen into ruin. He reported his discovery to the colonial authorities: they were the ruins of the city of Palenque, which later would be known as one of the leading Maya centers of the Classic period.

Beginning at the end of the eighteenth century, numerous scholars, explorers, architects, and lovers of travel and antiquities visited parts of Mexico, Guatemala, and Honduras. There they discovered the ruins of vast, sumptuous residential centers with monumental temples, palaces, streets, tombs, and steles, all erected by the members of a single civilization that had very ancient origins. The inhabitants of these palaces had created refined works of art. Above all, they had engraved the stones with symbols and very long inscriptions. Here was proof that the Maya civilization had truly reached an intellectually advanced level.

EXPLORERS AND TRAVELERS

Some of these explorers made interesting illustrations of the Maya sites they visited. Among the first was Count Jean-Frédérick Waldeck

An Interpretation of Maya Glyphs

Count Waldeck was among the first to study the puzzling Maya script incised on stone monuments. He patiently transcribed and studied the mysterious symbols. Interestingly, he transcribed many of  *them according to his own personal interpretation, as in this drawing, where some glyphs represent a stylized elephant head, a figment of the count's imagination.*

from Prague, who traveled extensively; on his long trips he stopped to study and draw the mysterious relics. Around 1825 he visited Palenque, Mayapán, Toniná, and Uxmal, where he made many lithographs that were used to illustrate Brasseur de Bourbourg's book *Ancient Monuments of Mexico and Palenque and Other Ruins* Count Waldeck's work is strange and interesting because instead of portraying objectively what he saw, he "interpreted" Maya art, modifying and enriching it with details borrowed from the Greek, Roman, and Egyptian worlds from which he believed Mesoamerican civilization was derived.

The most important scientific documents are the work of two nineteenth-century explorers who became famous for their research on the Maya: John Stephens, a young American lawyer, and Frederick Catherwood, an English artist. Eager to learn more about recent Mesoamerican discoveries, they took long exploratory trips in Yucatán and Honduras, chronicled their discoveries, and made drawings of all the major monuments.

Over the centuries the exploration and rediscovery of Maya sites was accompanied by a growing curiosity for the symbols engraved in

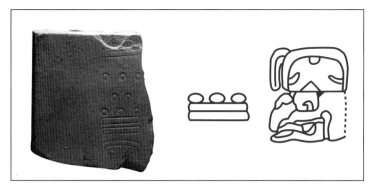

stone and painted on the few surviving manuscripts that were accidentally found in Europe. Before discussing the research that led to a true deciphering of the inscriptions, it is useful to place the Maya culture in a historical and chronological perspective, although today experts are still faced with enigmas and puzzles. The archaeological relics of what has been called the Maya civilization are scattered over a vast region that today encompasses five Central American countries: Mexico—where they are concentrated for the most part in the Yucatán Peninsula—Guatemala, Belize, Honduras, and El Salvador. The first excavation expeditions were launched between the end of the nineteenth and the early twentieth centuries. They followed proper scientific methods, and were headed by United States and Mexican archaeologists; among them was the Chichén Itzá expedition promoted by the Carnegie Institution of Washington, D.C. Since then, archaeological work in the Maya region has gradually expanded, but has yet to be completed.

The scholars have subdivided the history of this people up to the conquest into three phases: the Preclassic, Classic and Postclassic period. Each of these periods is in turn divided into an "early," "middle," and "late" period.

CHRONOLOGY

The Preclassic period spans from 2000 B.C. to A.D. 250. Although we still lack definitive data, most scholars believe that it was in the last phase of this period that the first groups of Maya ethnic stock formed close commercial ties with the Olmec people, whose ceremonial centers are still thought to be the most ancient in Mesoamerica. The Maya probably learned and adopted the calendrical system, the ball game, and the ritual of sacrifice—all topics that will be covered in this book—from the Olmec, considered the cultural matrix of Mesoamerica, and the Zapotec people. At the time, the Zapotec had already developed a form of writing, which has yet to be deciphered, which might well prove to be the forerunner of Maya as well as all other Mesoamerican writing systems.

The earliest Mayan ceremonial centers such as Uaxactún, Cerros, and El Mirador, recently

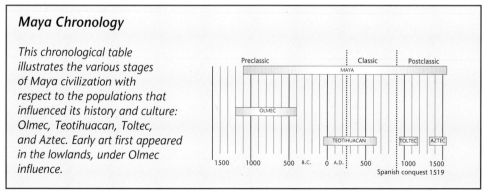

Maya Chronology

This chronological table illustrates the various stages of Maya civilization with respect to the populations that influenced its history and culture: Olmec, Teotihuacan, Toltec, and Aztec. Early art first appeared in the lowlands, under Olmec influence.

Preclassic · Classic · Postclassic
MAYA
OLMEC
TEOTIHUACAN · TOLTEC · AZTEC

1500 · 1000 · 500 B.C. · 0 A.D. · 500 · 1000 · 1500
Spanish conquest 1519

excavated in Belize, date back to this period. They consist of large pyramidal structures, some decorated with stucco masks, aligned with the four cardinal points and thought to serve as both temples and burial sites. In the Preclassic period there were no cities, only worship centers, with thatch and-mud huts clustered around them. Most likely, by then Maya society had attained a hierarchical structure, ruled by a chief who was also the high priest.

After 400 B.C., with the waning of the Olmec cultural influence, many ceremonial centers were expanded and the rural structures evolved into full-fledged urban structures, with administrative buildings and temple complexes. Some of these major centers are Kaminaljuyú and El Baúl in Guatemala, Izapa in Mexico, and Chalchuapa in El Salvador. In El Salvador, in addition to architecture, stone sculpture also flourished, in the form of steles and altars. The most ancient Maya hieroglyphic inscriptions were engraved on these as texts complementing the iconographies of famous individuals, celebrating their deeds, and reporting complex calendrical computations based on the Long Count system.

The growing expansion of several urban centers that began in the Preclassic period under the drive of the Olmec led to the birth of real city-states in the subsequent Classic period, which lasted from A.D. 250 to 900. It was at this time that Maya civilization reached its greatest political and cultural expansion.

Based on recent decoding of the hieroglyphics, some scholars have concluded that these city-states were not completely autonomous: at the height of the Classic period, they were grouped in two alliances, headed respectively by Tikal and Calakmul. They were probably military and diplomatic alliances entailing the payment of tributes and arranging marriages. Vari-

GULF OF MEXICO

CHICHÉN ITZÁ
MAYAPÁN
UXMAL
JAINA
TULUM

BAY OF CAMPECHE

MEXICO

LAMANAI
EL MIRADOR
RIO
ALTUNHA
AZUL
PALENQUE
TIKAL
BELIZE
PIEDRAS NEGRAS
YAXCHILÁN
BONAMPAK
CARACOL
ALTAR OF SACRIFICES
GULF OF
HONDURAS

GUATEMALA

QUIRIGUÁ
IZAPA
COPÁN
KAMINALJUYÚ
HONDURAS

PACIFIC OCEAN
EL SALVADOR

This map indicates the principal sites where Maya remains have been found, as well as some typical stylized finds of the various regions and periods.

ous factors contributed to the rapid development of Maya society. Most important was an agricultural system based on advanced methods and technologies. At the same time, there was a flourishing trade by land and waterways. In addition, the cultural influence engendered by contacts with the great center of Teotihuacan greatly contributed to this expansion.

During the Classic period, the kings who held centralized political, religious, and military power brought even greater lavishness to their courts to enhance their prestige in the eyes of the population. For this reason, they called upon their court artists, who created highly refined works of art. We can still admire the monumental sculptures, polychrome pottery, and ornaments of feathers and semiprecious stones they left behind.

What is even more surprising, though, is the extremely advanced knowledge the Maya achieved in astronomy, much like the cultures of Ancient Egypt and Mesopotamia. The oldest date inscribed on a Maya monument—found on Stele 29 in Tikal and corresponding to A.D. 292—is from the Classic period.

Thanks to the elaborate system of glyph writing that had been perfected in the Pre-

A beautiful statuette of an elegantly dressed man wearing a headdress and carrying a fan. Jaina style. An example of Classic period Maya ceramics. Brussels, Musées Royaux d'Art et d'Histoire.

classic age, the Maya rulers left an enduring testimony of their valor, victories, and battles, always marked by precise dates. The recent decoding of long inscriptions found on steles and other monuments in Tikal, Palenque, Copán, Quiriguá, and other centers has enabled researchers to at least partially reconstruct the history of the reigning dynasties.

A special caste of scribes was responsible for the task of setting to glyphs the astronomical and calendrical computations, oracles of the gods, and almanacs. They did this on long strips made of dried agave fibers, on which they painted the glyphs and corresponding illustrations. Unfortunately, almost no trace has survived of the precious historical documents that were destroyed at the time of the conquest.

The Maya cultural splendor and apogee followed the gradual political and cultural decline of many centers. Although Mayanists propose several theories, we still do not know the causes of this decline. Around 900, in the early Postclassic period, this weakening facilitated the arrival of new populations who moved in from northern Mexican regions. Following the Toltec invasion of the Yucatán Peninsula, several centers—Chichén Itzá, among them, and later Mayapán—flourished. These cities came under the rule of a new kind of political power, with a highly militarized social structure. New temples were built to the foreign god Quetzalcoatl—whom the Maya called Kukulkan—who soon supplanted the older deities. In 1250, with the fall of Mayapán, the last Yucatán capital, the centers of the Postclassic period fell apart because of invasions and internal strife. The Maya-Toltec empire disintegrated into several small kingdoms that were easy prey for the Spanish conquistadors.

The arch in Maya architecture

One typical element of Maya architecture was the so-called "false vault," or corbeled arch. Several buildings from different archaeological sites show that the arch evolved in the different regions and over time. Famous are the Labná (reproduced in the drawing) and the Kabán arches, both from the late Classic period.

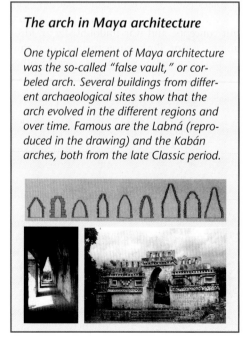

THE RIDDLE OF MAYA SCRIPT

Since the time of the Spanish conquest and in subsequent centuries, explorers have been fascinated not only by the imposing Maya architecture, but also by the strange signs they found engraved on stone monuments. The Franciscan bishop Diego de Landa was the first to be attracted to these mysterious glyphs. In 1566 he began to study these symbols and attempted to decipher them with the assistance of Maya Indians. He wrote down his efforts, which were to provide the key for decoding the Maya's script, however the manuscript laid forgotten until the latter part of the nineteenth century.

In 1864 de Landa's work, *Account of the Things of Yucatán,* was published for the first time by the French abbott Brasseur de Bourbourg. The manuscript recounted how the Spanish author had come to learn the written symbols for the solar calendar and its subdivisions into eighteen periods of twenty days each. Additionally, he had transcribed many glyphs into the Latin alphabet. Diego de Landa never succeeded in reading Maya script, limited as he was by his attempt to assign an alphabetic value to each glyph, that is, to find an equivalent for each glyph in the letters of the Latin alphabet. It was a flawed approach because, unlike all the other languages de Landa was familiar with, Maya script is not alphabet-based.

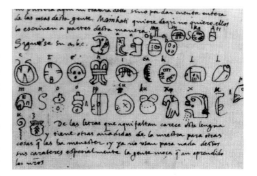

Diego de Landa was the first to attempt a transcription of Maya hieroglyphs. Because he mistakenly looked for a correspondence of each symbol with a Latin al-phabet letter, he was unsuccessful, since there are hundreds of Maya signs. It has now been established that in addition to having a phonetic value, the signs are also logograms.

De Landa's famous twenty-seven-character alphabet was analyzed in detail as a possible point of departure, but to no avail. Soon the scholars realized that de Landa had been deceived, for Maya script did not express sounds, but concepts, and was undoubtedly an ideographic script. Poring over the ancient manuscripts, scholars were able to decode other symbols that expressed calendrical symbols, numbers, and astronomical cycles.

Thus, they reached the conclusion that Maya writing was only concerned with mathematics and the calendar. This opinion, which took hold at the turn of the century, lasted until the end of the 1950s, and it was supported by several archaeologists, who believed the Maya had been an extremely quiet and

Symbols painted on codices were discovered much earlier than those found engraved and inscribed on stone monuments. Their style and content are very different: for the most part, codices contain astronomical, religious, and divinatory texts. This is a page from the Madrid Codex. *The glyphs are associated with images of gods and animals.*

contemplative people who devoted their time to religion and the study of the stars.

Until approximately fifty years ago, most of the Maya script had yet to be deciphered, thus our knowledge about their civilization was still very limited. In 1952, thanks to the Russian linguist Yuri Knorosov, a new approach was developed. Knorosov, trained as an Egyptologist, started with de Landa's "alphabet" and began to examine the surviving codices; he was able to identify approximately three hundred glyphs. He then realized that the number of signs was too small for the script to be an ideographic type, but the number was too large for the script to be a phonetic type. Thus Knorosov reached the conclusion that the Maya script was mixed—partly ideographic and partly phonetic—analogous to other early writings such as those of ancient Egypt and Mesopotamia.

However, unlike other phonetic writings, such as English, for example, Maya writing was based on syllables rather than on the individual letters of a genuine alphabet. This one fundamental element had eluded de Landa. As is often the case in the academic world, Knorosov's

Left: *Thanks to the patient work of the Russian-born American epigrapher Tatiana Proskouriakoff and other Russian, American, and European scholars, the inscriptions carved on Classic period stone monuments have been largely decoded. They are historical texts that contain the exact dates of the events they narrate.* Above: *Drawings of glyphs extrapolated from a text. Epigraphers were able to identify ideographic-type glyphs and phonetic-type glyphs.*

innovative theories were the subject of harsh criticism for several years. However, regardless of several mistakes he had made and several gaps in his decoding of the manuscripts, the theory that phonetic elements were part of the Maya script have proven to be correct.

RECENT DISCOVERIES

In 1958 Heinrich Berlin, an epigrapher who had been studying the Palenque slabs for many years, reached a new breakthrough in decoding the script. He noticed that several sets of glyphs archaeologists had discovered at different sites all shared a common element. More precisely, each set contained a main character, which though unique to each site, included one single prefix that was common to these special glyphs. This meant that although each glyph had a different meaning, they all had the same function. Berlin called these new types of glyphs he had identified "emblem glyphs." He understood them to indicate the name of the city or of the ruling family. It was the first step toward the

A stone slab covered with Maya hieroglyphics from the Classic period, part of a group of slabs found in 1787 in Palenque by the Spanish captain Antonio del Río. Madrid, Museo de América.

realization that the Maya script was not simply limited to denoting calendrical or mathematical terms.

At the beginning of the 1960s, the Russian-born archaeologist and architect Tatiana Proskouriakoff brought an unexpected innovation to the decoding of the script. She was the first to establish, with absolute certainty, that the inscriptions found at the Maya sites had a historical content. In examining several steles from the ancient city of Piedras Negras, Proskouriakoff noticed the regular recurrence of dates that identified periods of approximately sixty years each, and seemed to correspond to the average length of a human life. The first date seemed to correspond to the time of birth; after approximately twenty years, there was a date marking the ascent to the throne. Other dates marked events such as wars or marriages, and the last date coincided with the time of death. Almost all the inscriptions

Even ceramic vessels, such as this Classic bowl, contain religious or mythological inscriptions. The bowl is decorated with glyphs in a spiral design. Brussels, Musées Royaux d'Art et d'Histoire.

were associated with relief images of individuals who most certainly had been kings, queens, princes, or dignitaries.

The decoding of the Piedras Negras, and later of the Yaxchilán, steles led to the positive conclusion that the Maya had not simply narrated myths or reported calendar information, such as the narratives of the handwritten codices. Indeed, they had also narrated true historical accounts of the life and events of the ruling dynasties of the period when their civilization reached its highest point, the Classic period.

Thanks to the work of Knorosov, Berlin, and especially, Proskouriakoff, scholars were slowly able to reconstruct the history and chronology of several ancient Maya centers, including the rulers who succeeded each other, the wars, and the alliances of the various city-states. Unlike the study and deciphering of other ancient writings, such as the Mycenaean "Linear B" syllabary and Egyptian hieroglyphics, the Maya script has only recently begun to shed its veil of mystery.

As of today, approximately eighty percent of the glyphs have been decoded, however we are still far from having reached the end of this fascinating research. A few American scholars, for example Linda Schele, David Stuart, David Freidel, David Kelley, and Michael Coe, as well as such European scholars as Nikolai Grube, have made their contribution and are still working today to attempt to solve the Mayan puzzle.

Two examples of writing support: stone steles covered with glyphs. As in other cases, these are commemorative monuments with historical dates and events. The stele on the right contains a Long Count date corresponding to A.D. 737. Private collection; Brussels, Musées Royaux d'Art et d'Histoire.

THE DOCUMENTS

The stone inscriptions that the Maya have left to posterity appear especially on steles, altars, flights of steps, and other monuments. The narratives that scholars were able to decode are mostly historical; in particular, they had the purpose of exalting the deeds of royal family members. In fact, it was possible to arrive at a precise reconstruction of the chronology of the narrated events because the events are always accompanied by their dates of occurrence. Conversely, the major written sources for astronomical knowledge, mythology, and religion are the pre-Columbian codices—texts written in Maya that were translated into Latin by native scribes after the conquest—and other documents written directly by Spanish clerics. Unfortunately, only four of these Maya codices have survived. Practically all of

Detail from a Dresden Codex *page, with numerous glyphs, including numerical ones consisting of bars and dots. At the bottom are three major deities of the Maya pantheon: on the left, the death god with skeletal features; in the center, the young maize god; on the right, the North Star god, guardian of merchants and cocoa.*

Mythology and Astrology

Detail from a Dresden Codex *page. This mythological scene is painted in vivid colors and shows Yum Kaax, the young maize god, holding a vase as he approaches the death god. The maize god wears an ear of corn, while the death god wears a skull.*

this precious literary heritage was destroyed at the time of the conquest, for the conquistadors believed such native works were diabolical.

The term "codex" refers to a manuscript usually written on paper-like material made from the beaten bark of the ficus tree or from agave fibers. The Aztec and the Mixtec also used deerskin. The long strips, folded accordion-style, were enclosed in rigid wood or leather covers; the text was written on both sides of the sheet and decorated with illustrations painted in rich colors. While the Aztec codices are for the most part pictographic with some syllabic elements, Maya codices have pictograms alternating with glyphs of the syllabic type.

Of the four, the *Dresden Codex* is probably the most ancient, having been written between approximately 1200 and 1250, at the height of the Postclassic period. It consists of an agave-fiber strip, 141 inches (358 cm) long, folded into 78 sides, and almost completely filled with script. The text is a collection of astronomical and astrological almanacs that are extremely important for an understanding of Mayan knowledge. The codex tables describing the eclipses and the cycle of Venus show a highly developed level of scientific knowledge; they were possibly copied around 1200 from a more ancient text of the Classic period. Other sections of the text, such as those that recount prophecies for the new year and predictions about the harvest, belong to a later period.

The *Paris Codex*, also known as the *Peresianus Codex*, unfortunately has survived only in fragments: only eleven sides of the strip remain; it is almost certainly slightly more recent than the *Dresden Codex*. Most of the text refers to a calendar period of eleven *katun* (one *katun* equals twenty years). The painted illustrations depict a number of deities, and the glyphs illustrate prophecies and sacred rituals. Perhaps the most interesting element is a zodiac; unfortunately, only parts of it remain. Unlike the other codices, this one had several annotations in Latin characters from the post-Columbian era, but they are now illegible.

The *Madrid Codex,* also known as the *Tro-Cortesianus Codex,* actually consists of two fragments discovered at different times and in two different locations in Spain. The scholar Léon Rosny was the first to realize they were fragments of the same manuscript. The text of the two fragments consists of fifty-six pages that have been dated to a late period, between 1300 and 1400.

Unlike the other codices, this text does not recount astronomical or calendrical matters. It contains almanacs and predictions about everyday activities, and indicates a level of scientific knowledge that is just below that of the earlier codices. The fourth document, known as the *Grolier Codex,* is a recent discovery: its fragments contain an astronomical text about the Venusian cycle.

In addition to the four codices, there are two written sources of the epic-mythological type that are ex-

Codex Writing

The Postclassic period saw the disappearance of steles inscribed with a mostly ideographic script, replaced by mostly phonetic signs. The four extant codices are written in phonetic glyphs that are more difficult to decipher and interpret, a sign that writing had become the domain of a restricted intellectual caste.

tremely important aids in the reconstruction, at least partially, of Maya religious thought and the historical traditions of the Postclassic period. They are the *Popol Vuh* and *The Books of Chilam Balam.*

The *Popol Vuh* (which literally means "the book of counsel") is essentially a kind of biblical text of the Maya people. It contains a number of myths and events narrated in the form of legends—undoubtedly based on true historical events—although they cannot be confirmed, about the origins of one specific Maya lineage, the Quiché from Guatemala. In all likelihood, an educated clerk who had inherited the tradition of the ancient scribes wrote the original text in glyphs in

Page fragment from the Paris Codex, *with cosmogonic figures and gods. This codex contains the only surviving Maya zodiac, though only in fragments.*

the sixteenth century. After the conquest, it disappeared. Luckily, several centuries later a copy transcribed into Latin characters was found, and it was translated into Spanish by the abbott Brasseur de Bourbourg.

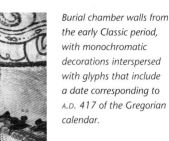

Burial chamber walls from the early Classic period, with monochromatic decorations interspersed with glyphs that include a date corresponding to A.D. 417 of the Gregorian calendar.

The Books of Chilam Balam, on the other hand, consist of a number of Yucatec manuscripts, also transcribed into Latin characters during the colonial period, probably by descendants of Maya priests who had jealously guarded their ancestors' esoteric knowledge. The literal meaning of Chilam Balam is "jaguar priest." This work contains very interesting information about medicine, astrology, and astronomy, as well as historical and religious information about the Yucatec region before the arrival of the Europeans. In comparing the Chilam Balam to the Dresden Codex, it appears likely that the Chilam Balam was also based on ancient pre-Columbian codices, as evidenced by analogies found in both texts referring to the tun and katun calendar cycles.

After this brief review of epigraphic and manuscript sources, we should add that the Maya also used ceramic as a medium of text narration. In the past twenty years several scholars, Michael Coe among them, have studied the glyphs painted on vases and bowls that illustrate complex scenes of everyday life at court, as well as encounters and battles between human beings, gods, and animals. Maya inscriptions also appear on wall frescoes and are incised on objects made of various materials such as wood, bone, and semi-precious stones.

The Leiden Plate

Glyph that introduces the initial series

8 baktun

14 katun

3 tun
Fish

1 uinal

12 kin

1 eb

5° Man of the Night

Yaxkin

title or name

Chan

Ascension

rise (to the throne)

Balam Ahau

emblematic glyph

Illustration of the Leiden Plate (right)

The Leiden Plate is a precious Maya find, now preserved in the Dutch city of Leiden. It is a jadeite pendant eight and a half inches (22 cm) high, inscribed on both sides. One side depicts a stylized high-ranking official, most likely King Moon Zero Bird; the other side is inscribed with many tiny glyphs that express a date corresponding to A.D. 320. Leiden, Rijksmuseum voor Volkenkunde.

LANGUAGE AND GRAPHIC SYSTEM

Today, several million Maya Indians still live in the regions that saw the flourishing of the ancient Maya civilization. Although it appears likely that in the past only one Maya language was spoken in the various parts of the region, today approximately thirty idioms derived from a single stock survive and are spoken over a vast area.

The system of writing decoded by the scholars belongs to the Classic period. According to the most widely accepted theory, this writing expressed the Cholan language of the southern Maya region and the Yucatec language of the northern Maya. The four pre-Columbian manuscript codices are written in Yucatec.

Thanks to the difficult work of decoding the epigraphic texts and the manuscripts, we can now easily read most of the written symbols of the Classic period, although the interpretation of many of them is still a subject of doubt and controversy. We should keep in mind that since the deciphering is fairly recent, it is possible that many interpretations that we take for granted today could be modified in the future.

Although at the dawn of the Preclassic age the Olmec culture strongly influenced Maya civilization, the Maya did not inherit their language. In all probability, the Olmec spoke a language of Mixe-Zoquean stock, which is totally different from the Mayan linguistic family. However, many scholars believe that the symbols that constitute the basis of the Mayan script are derived from Olmec and Zapotec symbols. We will discuss this problem, which has yet to be resolved, later in more detail.

Usually an inscription engraved on a stele consists of several rows of signs of varying length, generally written in vertical columns and meant to be read from left to right and from top to bottom. Symbols are called glyphs, a word derived from the Greek *gliphein,* which literally means "to engrave, to carve." Each glyph consists of a central element and one or more associated elements appended to it, which form an elaborate design, usually in the form of a rectangular or oval scroll.

What do these elegant, miniature designs express? Letters, sounds, images, abstract concepts? The riddle seemed impossible to solve. The key to breaking the Mayan code was found only after scholars were able to solve the puzzle of identifying to which system (ideographic or alphabetical) the script belonged. Thanks to the epigraphic research done by Yuri Knorosov, scholars were finally able to determine that it was a mixed script, and for this reason, extremely elaborate. It is, in fact, a logo-syllabic system consisting of glyphs that are logograms (where each symbol expresses a complete word) or ideograms (where each symbol expresses a thing or an idea) and by other glyphs that are syllabic.

The greatest problem the decoders faced was that it was possible to write each word in more than one way, without changing the word's meaning. Moreover, different glyphs could be used to extrapolate the syllables. One typical, easy to understand example is the glyph for the word *jaguar, balam* in Maya, which is often found as an element of names of rulers (Shield Jaguar, Bird Jaguar, Snake Jaguar).

The scribe could simply write the word by using a logogram—that is, by drawing the head of a jaguar, or even the whole

Painted vase from a Tikal tomb, showing a king and a servant, and a glyph text.

Two stucco glyphs dated between A.D. 600 and 900, with both animal and human figures. Madrid, Museo de América.

silhouette of the animal. He could also choose a syllabic system, and write "jaguar" by using a glyph consisting of three syllables: *ba-la-ma*. The last *a* was silent. A third possibility was to mix the syllabic and logographic methods within the same word. The result was that the image of the jaguar's head was now between the syllables *ba* and *ma* in place of the second syllable; some scholars refer to this system as "riddle script."

A complicating factor was the fact that several words were expressed with glyphs that had the same pronunciation, although their meanings differed. One typical example is the word *chan*, which translates the terms for "snake" and "sky" as well as the number four.

The Guardian Gods of Writing

The Maya worshiped the guardian gods of writing and the scribes who possessed writing knowledge. Scribes formed a restricted high caste, possibly distinct from that of the priests. Their task was to record on stone the king's actions and the heavenly cycles, and to write mythological and oracular texts on codices. Here rabbit god, from a painted eighth-century A.D. vase, is shown in the act of writing with a brush on a folded codex lined with jaguar skin. The monkey was another guardian deity of writing.

Simply put, there were three different glyphs that referred to three concepts that were unrelated to each other, although the pronunciation was the same. A similar example is that of the terms for "vulture," "torch," and "bundle of sticks": the word *ta*—which in the Cholan dialect also refers to a locative preposition—was used to express all three meanings.

The numbers from one to nineteen were written using a system of dots and bars. We will discuss them later in the book. In addition, to each number corresponded a glyph, called "portrait variable" (or "head variable"), composed of a stylized head, possibly the image of an ancient deity.

Overall, the present state of research indicates that the Maya system of writing contained a much higher number of logographic glyphs than of syllabic-phonetic glyphs.

Syntactically, the sentences reconstructed from historical texts on steles had the following structure: "He captured—Jeweled Skull—Bird Jaguar," which in our language would correspond to: "Bird Jaguar captured Jeweled Skull." Hence, the sentence structure, consisting of verb—object—subject, is unusual for us.

The proper names of the Maya rulers are still an enigma; archaeologists have named them based on the glyphs associated with their images. The names of rulers were always complemented by glyphs representing the cities over which they ruled, in addition to other suffixes that expressed honorary titles such as "the divine." Honorary titles were preceded by the *ah* proclitic prefix, while the female corresponding prefix was *na*.

As of this date, there has been great progress has been made in decoding the Maya script, thanks in large part to the experts we have mentioned. They have succeeded in interpreting the meaning of numerous nouns, verbs, adjectives, and place names, and they have identified the grammatical and syntactic structure of sentences. These studies are very recent, and in the future, they may help widen our knowledge of Maya culture and thought. Questions about the origins of the Maya script, however, remain, as do its relations to the other graphic systems of Mesoamerica that have yet to be decoded. The search goes on, and these issues are still a long way from being resolved.

Like those shown on the preceding page, this stucco glyph has yet to be decoded. It was found in Palenque and dates from the Classic period. Madrid, Museo de América.

As we pointed out, the most ancient glyphs used to express the Maya language graphically are associated with calendrical computations and express numbers and dates. Several scholars agree in looking for the origin of the glyphs to the Zapotec civilization, which had its center in Monte Albán, in the Mexican region of Oaxaca. The antiquity of the glyphs incised on the stone monuments of Monte Albán (only the numerical and calendrical glyphs have been decoded so far), leads us to believe that the Zapotec script is the ancestor of the script later adopted by the Maya people. It is possible, in turn, that the Zapotec inherited their graphic system from the Olmec, who were their predecessors; however, we do not have sufficient evidence to confirm this theory. There is also scant evidence for the claim that the Maya script may have spread to other civilizations, such as that of Teotihuacan, of the same period.

Unfortunately, for reasons that have yet to be discovered, at the end of the Classic period the Maya stopped erecting engraved steles. They left no information about the dynasties that ruled Yucatec cities such as Uxmal and Sayil, or the last Maya-Toltec cities of the Postclassic period. Possibly, their kings, now subjected to a dominant foreign people, refused to hand down their secret knowledge. In that period, only manuscripts with an astronomic, religious, or divinatory content were written, and we presume writing had become a secret tool, the province of a restricted intellectual elite. There is active, ongoing archaeological and epigraphic research on the subject, and probably more secrets of the Maya script will be unveiled in the near future.

Puzzle Writing

The complex nature of Maya writing, which some scholars have dubbed "puzzle writing," is given by the fact that it includes ideographic symbols and syllabic-phonetic symbols, often written together to strengthen a word's meaning. Here are some easily understandable examples:

1) Balám (jaguar)—ideographic
2) Ba-Balám—phonetic-ideographic
3) Ba-la-ma—phonetic
4) Verb translated as "battling" or "fighting."
5) "Lord of Copán," used as a symbolic glyph for the Honduran city
6) As with many other forms of writing, glyphs are read from left to right and from top to bottom

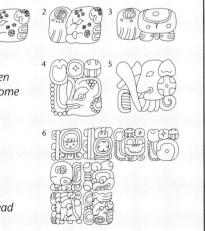

THE MAYA TODAY

Today, descendants of the same populations that were once subdued by the Spanish conquistadors inhabit the territories scattered with the remains of the ancient Maya civilization. There are approximately three million people, grouped in nine ethnic groups, the most numerous and important of which are the Quiché and the Yucatec. The Lacandón Maya, only a few hundred of which survive today, are considered the true heirs and custodians of the ancient culture and ancestral traditions of the Classic period. From the linguistic point of view, approximately thirty dialects exist today, which probably descended from the same stock.

The major characteristic of today's Maya is the syncretism of their pre-Hispanic cultural and religious traditions, which they never shed, and the European-derived traditions imposed by the colonizers. In many churches, during religious holidays the Catholic liturgy is complemented by, sometimes intertwined with, other, more ancient rituals, and the saints are worshiped together with ancestral deities. Shamanism and nahualism are still widely practiced in several regions by healing witch doctors, from time immemorial jealous custodians of the arts of divination and medicine.

Today, the basic nucleus of Maya society is the family, which is also the center of all household and productive activities. As at the beginning of the Classic period, agriculture constitutes the basis of the present-day Mayan economy. In addition to maize, which is the main crop, they farm squash, beans, and several kinds of vegetables, mostly for local consumption. They also grow export products such as coffee and sugar cane, which they export to Europe.

Among their many craft activities, weaving stands out. The techniques for making textiles and clothing have changed only slightly over time, and still resemble the methods depicted in ancient iconographies. For example, today women still us the belt loom, identical to the type in use during the Classic period, as represented in Jaina art. Men, for the most part, use other types of looms, such as the vertical loom and the pedal loom, imported from Spain. Unlike their ancestors, who used only cotton and agave fibers, today's weavers also use sheep's wool, which was unknown to the Indians before the arrival of Columbus.

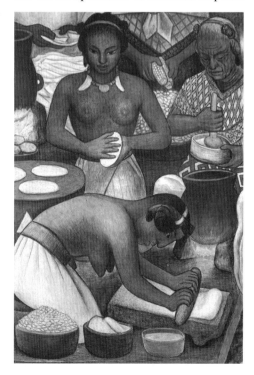

Above: *A painted plate from the late Classic period, with a scene from daily Maya life one still sees today: a woman preparing corn meal on a milling stone* (metate).

Left: *A famous mural by Mexican artist Diego Rivera shows women preparing tortillas.*

LIFE AT COURT

The experts who are working at decoding
the Maya script have unveiled for us the life
and actions of previously unknown kings and
queens who ruled the Maya city-states and
lived in lavish palaces, surrounded by dignitaries
and priests. The ceramics, jewels, wall paintings,
and reliefs evoke for us the world of the
Maya courts and their civil and religious
rituals and ceremonies.

SCENES OF PALACE LIFE

At the end of the 1950s, the history of Maya cities and their inhabitants was still a riddle. It was at this time that several experts detected the frequent and regular recurrence of precise symbols, carved on the stones of the major archaeological sites. They called these symbols "emblem glyphs" and reached the conclusion that they referred to the name of the city, or even the state of which the city dominated. Since then, several other emblematic glyphs have been identified, including those of less-known ceremonial centers such as Caracol, Altun Ha, Toniná, and Tamarindito.

In the 1960s, thanks to the patient work of Tatiana Proskouriakoff, scholars were able to decode and read entire inscriptions they found engraved on steles discovered next to the archaeological sites of Yaxchilán and Piedras Negras. Proskouriakoff's work is fundamental because it led to an important discovery: unlike the texts painted in the codices, those carved on stones and slabs contained exact dates that referred to events that had really happened and to high-ranking individuals who had really existed.

Building on the work accomplished so far, scholars have been able to identify many of the dignitaries whose likeness is engraved on the steles and who appear decorated with lavish headdresses, feathers, and jewels. Their names, such as Eighteen Rabbit, Noble Cacao (Ah Cacao), and Stormy Sky, evoke in us a sense of wonder and curiosity.

Hence from the most ancient inscriptions, such as that inscribed on Stele 29 from Tikal, which has been dated to A.D. 292, we learn that at the beginning of the Classic period the Maya lands saw the rise of

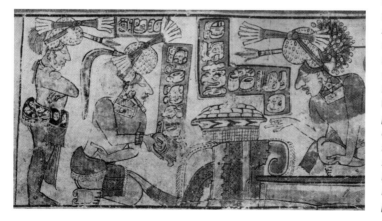

Two painted scenes from vases offer an accurate description of court life in the Classic period. **Above:** *A parade of hunters wear conical hats and carry a deer, whose meat was prized by the Maya.* **Below:** *Two individuals, probably ambassadors, deferentially offer a basket filled with food to the king seated before them. The large headdresses denote high rank. Glyphs are also painted in the scene.*

true city-states run by a centralized and efficient political and social system. Each state was ruled by a religious and administrative center, within an urban structure. Next to the temples stood the palaces where the king lived with his many wives and children, surrounded by an aristocratic elite of dignitaries and priests.

Written documents tell us that distinct and rigid social classes existed, together with different professional categories, the most important of these being merchants, craftsmen, musicians, and scribes. The king, who was also commander-in-chief of the army, ruled with absolute power and succession to the throne was hereditary. Thus, power was transmitted from father to son.

The inscriptions recount in great chronological detail the major events in the life of each ruler: his birth, accession to the throne, marriage, battles with his enemies, and death. From these texts emerges an important general aspect of Maya and Mesoamerican culture: each event, each daily action or ritual was strictly connected to calendrical cycles, to the movement of the stars and the planets and, of course, to the will of the gods.

We find proof of the rulers' power not only in the symbols and reliefs inscribed in stone, but also in the rich funeral furnishings discovered in such tombs as that of King Pacal in Palenque. According to a widespread belief common to many ancient civilizations, the deceased would continue to enjoy luxury, glory, and happiness in the afterlife.

Even today, the better-preserved archaeological sites permit us to appreciate the stately quality of the royal palaces and religious buildings of the ancient Maya cities, built to exalt the almost divine power of their rulers. Each ceremonial center had unique features as evident in the great variety of architectural styles and the refined decorative elements.

Nevertheless, how did the mysterious decline of Maya civilization, which was already complete by the time of the conquest, come about? The more reliable theories entertain the possibility that frequent and bloody wars came to weaken the power of each city-state. Alternatively, that the populations rebelled against the absolute power of their rulers, leading to civil wars and the fall of the reigning dynasties. Some scholars believe instead that the decline was due to demographic and economic reasons.

There are not answers to these questions as of yet, even though a careful analysis of the steles' inscribed glyphs has allowed us to expand greatly our knowledge of Maya civilization. Thus, these more specifically historical inscriptions have added to our understanding of the astronomical and religious texts contained in the codices.

Above: *A stunning incense burner, in the form of a man, made of painted terra-cotta, from Copán. It was found among a group of votive objects near the Scribe's Tomb.*
Right: *The Castillo, a temple in the city of Tulum, Yucatán, one of the last Maya strongholds after the destruction of Mayapán.*

COPÁN

Several elements make up the Copán glyph: on the left is the glyph for "blood," on top two marks indicate "lord," and in the center is the image of a bat with a marked snout.

Copán, a spectacular Maya archaeological site, lies in present-day Honduras. The ceremonial center covers a vast surface of almost forty acres (16 ha). The acropolis consists of a vast platform on which rise several pyramid-shaped temples, along with palaces and three central courts. The most interesting building is the Temple of the Hieroglyphic Stairway, whose summit is reached by climbing a monumental staircase consisting of sixty-three risers totally covered with 2,500 glyphs.

The court used for ball games (the spheristerion) is the most interesting and complete of the Maya archaeological sites excavated so far. A paved rectangular field, it is in the shape of a capital I, open on the southern side and closed on the opposite side by a flight of steps. It is decorated by a unique element, not found elsewhere: three stone heads representing the Ara parrot, a bird which was probably connected to the worship of the moving daylight sun. Ball playing, a practice of several pre-Columbian Mesoamerican peoples, was a ritual rather than a sport. We will discuss its importance in a later chapter.

The extremely large number of steles and monolithic altars enriched by low and high relief sculptures are very important to the experts trying to reconstruct the history of Copán. Each stele bears the portrait of a ruler, always accompanied by inscriptions that relate his history and deeds. Crafted with a refined, richly detailed technique and cosmogonic details, they are almost baroque in style.

The four walls of Altar Q are in all probability a celebration of the reigning Copán dynasty. Sixteen richly attired kings are shown in the reliefs: as in a procession, they are sitting cross-legged and next to each king is a glyph indicating his name. In analyzing the text it was found that beginning in A.D. 400, the monarchs of this city-state were all members of the same family. Certainly, this continuity contributed to the economic and cultural expansion of Copán that lasted up to the end of the Classic period. One stele, which has been dated to 810, celebrated the prestige of a ruler who promoted the artistic and economic development of the city, and who was named "New Sun on the Horizon."

At that time Copán, like many other Maya centers, entered a period of decline that marked the end of the powerful ancient city-states.

This stunning Copán stele is a portrait of Eighteen Rabbit, one of the most charismatic rulers of the Classic period.

CARACOL

Caracol has only recently begun to reveal its ancient secrets. It was probably the leading Maya city in the geographic area that today corresponds to the country of Belize, and which is rich in archaeological remains.

Maya-language people, constituting approximately ten percent of the country's population, live in present-day Belize, a country located between Mexico, Guatemala, and the Atlantic Coast.

Several archaeological sites have been excavated, but due to the lack of adequate roads, only a small number of them is accessible to the public. The remains of what was probably the largest Maya city in Belize, Caracol, lie in the southwestern part of the country, on the slopes of a hilly range, near the border with Guatemala. A group of archaeologists from the University of Pennsylvania discovered the site for the first time in 1958. Since then, several excavations have brought to light fifty monuments, including several tombs of dignitaries, stone cisterns for the collection of water, steles, and altars.

Many of these monuments have features that are unique to this site: they are circular and the stone inscriptions are huge. One of the temple pyramids is very high, and its area at the base is even larger than that of Tikal, the grandiose Maya center located approximately forty-four miles (70 km) from Caracol.

The large number of terraces still visible around Caracol are evidence that intensive farming was practiced in the area for many centuries. Caracol's geographic location and the existence of crystal rock caves nearby also helped to increase its importance as a commercial center.

Deciphering the inscriptions at this site has enabled scholars to identify the stages of the city's historical development and the various rulers of its reigning dynasty. Caracol flourished at the height of the Classic period; it began to reach its apogee around the year 485, and began its decline around 800.

The imposing ruins of the Canaa Temple in Caracol. More than fifty monuments have been unearthed since the first 1958 excavation by University of Pennsylvania archaeologists.

PALENQUE

To the left are two emblematic glyphs associated with Palenque, one of the most prestigious Maya cities which flourished in large part thanks to King Pacal, who is buried under the Temple of the Inscriptions.

The archaeological site of Palenque is located in the Mexican state of Chiapas, near the Usumacinta River Valley. Like Tikal's monuments, those of Palenque were found and excavated in the heart of a dense tropical forest.

The large, elaborate ceremonial center covers a surface of approximately six square miles (16 sq. km), but only the central part is accessible to visitors. This central part contains four major temples and a large complex referred to as the palace, whose function has yet to be identified. It is composed of a rectangular platform on which several structures are arranged around interior courtyards. The most interesting element of this architectural complex is a four-story square tower, which many believe served as an astronomical observatory.

The group of religious buildings includes the Temple of the Sun and the Temple of the Cross, along with a third temple, called the Temple of the Foliate Cross. The temples were named after the cosmogonic symbols found in the richly colored stucco reliefs—including the Tree of Life, the Solar Disc, and the Maize Leaf—that decorate the walls of the various halls. These particular symbols were central to Maya religion; their representation had a precise significance within the context of the ceremonial center. The sacred building that rises imposingly over the central area is the famous Temple of the Inscriptions; its pyramid is covered by three large panels decorated with hundreds of glyphs.

In 1952 an important discovery shed new light on Maya archaeology. Under the base of the temple, at a depth of some seventy feet (22 m), the sumptuous burial chamber of a king who ruled Palenque from A.D. 615 to 683 was excavated. It was the tomb of King Kin Pacal,

the Sun Shield, whose funeral furnishings contained a precious mask of jade mosaic and several jewels. For the first time, archaeologists realized that the great pyramids were not only places of worship, but also funeral monuments.

1) Temple of the Inscrip- tions
2) Palace Tower
3) Palace
4) Ball Court (spheristerion)
5) North Group
6) Temple of the Cross
7) Temple of the Foliate Cross
8) Temple of the Sun

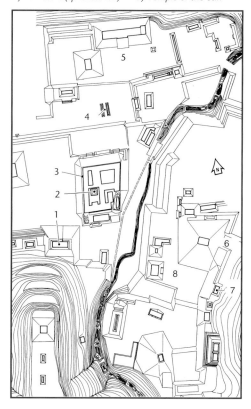

PIEDRAS NEGRAS

The Maya inscriptions of the altars and steles of Piedras Negras were among the first to be deciphered. The reliefs revealed the deeds and rituals of the ancient rulers.

The region of Petén covers a vast area in present-day Guatemala. From the earliest times, its historical and cultural development and its events were especially affected by the history of nearby Mexico and Belize. In almost inaccessible areas of the tropical forest lie the remains of important Maya ceremonial centers, Tikal being the best known of these. On the right bank, in a bend of the Usumacinta River, lies the Piedras Negras site, which is now only accessible by boat. This large river, at the time an important communication and commercial waterway, fertilized the surrounding alluvial plain creating rich farmland, thus contributing to the development of Piedras Negras as well as other contemporaneous centers in the same region.

The first archaeologists who ventured into the tropical forest and came upon the ruins of Piedras Negras in the 1930s found the ancient buildings in very poor condition, protected as they were only by roofs of wood and thatch. Three building groups were identified: the most imposing of them consists of three pyramid-shaped temples and of palaces arranged around three interior courtyards.

The importance of the site lies in the large number and particularly high artistic level of the stone sculptures. These consist for the most part of large steles and wall panels decorated in low relief with human figures and in high relief with depictions of the kings who took turns in ruling the city, together with their wives, nobles, and prisoners.

One unique feature of the Piedras Negras sculptures is that the individuals are shown sitting in a frontal position. The steles have many inscriptions that were decoded thanks to Proskouriakoff's work. These inscriptions narrate the lives of seven reigning dynasties; the steles narrating the same political event were grouped close to the same temple. The decoded inscriptions cover a period of time extending from A.D. 618 to the end of the eighth century, when most likely another center came to dominate the surrounding areas.

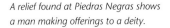

A relief found at Piedras Negras shows a man making offerings to a deity.

TIKAL

Several emblematic glyphs were used to denote the city of Tikal, in present-day Guatemala, possibly the largest and most powerful city of the Classic period. The glyphs recount the history of its many kings.

In the thick tropical forest of Petén in Guatemala, even today Tikal's impressive ruins bespeak the prestige enjoyed by this city.

The more ancient buildings have been dated to the closing centuries of the Preclassic period, though the city developed as an urban center proper between A.D. 200 and 300, as evidenced by the first stele, which has been dated to 292.

The city was ruled by many kings, among them Noble Cacao (also known as Ruler A) and Stormy Sky. Thanks to their skillful exploitation of the surrounding farmland and the development of commercial waterways and roads, in all probability Tikal grew into a city of about forty thousand people. From a simple ceremonial center, it grew into a true city-state with an extended urban structure.

The archaeological site, which covers a surface of approximately six square miles (16 sq. km), includes almost one thousand buildings, in addition to hundreds of engraved steles. The numerous building and temple complexes were connected by a network of paved roads, or causeways, decorated with stuccoes, called *sacbeob* (literally, "white road"). There were also large areas with a spheristerion for playing ball, markets, steam baths, and centers for the study of the sky and its phenomena. Two twin pyramids, one of them approximately 120 feet (40 m) high, towered over a central square in the heart of the city. The architectural structure of these prestigious places of worship consisted of three parts. First came a pyramid-shaped platform with a flight of wide steps, reachable by a steep staircase; on top was the temple proper and, finally, an ornamental roof comb. Carved and painted stucco masks in bright colors, which today have washed out, decorated the whole complex.

The prestigious level of architecture, the vastness of the urban complex, and the information gathered from the inscriptions all point to the existence of a strictly organized, tightly held political, administrative, and religious rule. As with most Maya centers, however, the fact that no steles were erected datable later than the year 900 means that by then the decline and abandonment of the site had begun. The reasons for such decline are still unknown.

Above: *A funeral mask in jade, pyrite, and shells, from Tikal funeral furnishings.*
Left: *Tikal, group of temples in the north acropolis.*

YAXCHILÁN

The Yaxchilán glyphs, together with those of Piedras Negras, were among the first to be decoded. They recount many deeds of kings such as Shield Jaguar and Bird Jaguar.

The city of Yaxchilán flourished on the left bank of the Usumacinta River, its historical and cultural development being similar t o that of other centers in the same valley, for example, Piedras Negras, Quiriguá, and Seibal. One building complex is located on a terrace next to the riverbank, while others are arranged on the overlooking hilly slopes. These include two acropolises of different sizes.

Particularly elegant elements of Yaxchilán's architecture are the majestic stairs dug into the rock of the terrace slopes on which the temples rise. They serve as natural platforms, similar to the man-made ones found at other Maya sites. The buildings are, for the most part, rectangular, arranged around a patio, and usually topped by large roof combs decorated with fretwork.

Here also, as at Piedras Negras, the images and inscriptions carved in stone enabled archaeologists to reconstruct the historical events of the city and the individuals who ruled it. Unfortunately, most of the steles located next to the temples are no longer readable due to deterioration from time and humidity. The stone lintels of the buildings, however, are in a good state of conservation and provide excellent artistic and historical documentation.

From the events narrated in the glyphs and their dates, we learn that the city flourished during the Classic period, reaching its apogee

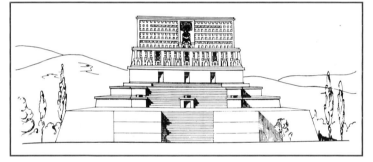

under the rule of Kings Shield Jaguar and Bird Jaguar, between 700 and 800. At the time Yaxchilán became the most powerful center in the Usumacinta Valley, and was able to annex a large part of the surrounding territory as a result of victorious wars. However, the monuments bear no dates after 808: it was probably at that time that a sudden decline in military and political set in.

The lovely low and high reliefs depict war scenes, prisoners being sacrificed, kings and their wives offering their self-sacrifice to the gods. All around these images are celestial and cosmological symbols.

Most Yaxchilán palaces were rectangular and built around a long inside courtyard, as in the diagram below. They were decorated with elegant latticework roof combs.

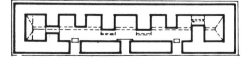

CHICHÉN ITZÁ

Very few inscriptions from Chichén Itzá survive, although it was one of the last great Maya cities. In fact, the custom of narrating political and military deeds through inscriptions was lost in the Postclassic period.

Chichén Itzá came to have a dominant role from the years 1000 to 1200 in the Postclassic period; its military and cultural strength extended over other Yucatán centers.

From the excavations and the few precious surviving historical Maya sources, archaeologists have been able to establish that the city expanded rapidly thanks to the migration of Toltec peoples from the north. The new ruling class forced a new culture, new traditions, and the cult of Kukulkan, the hero-god, on the autochthonous tribes of the Puuc region.

In the grandiose archaeological complex of Chichén Itzá, located between today's Cancún and Mérida, we can admire the fusion of Maya and Toltec art. The architecture of these Postclassic buildings still bears traces of Maya-style decorations, however the overall effect is somewhat austere, with none of the gay elegance of the earlier ages that we admire in, for example, the Casa Colorada. The importance of the new cult of Kukulkan is clear from the many sculptures of this god, represented as a feathered serpent.

Several architectural elements in Chichén Itzá provide evidence that the Toltec were a war-mongering society engrossed in cruel rituals. The *chacmool,* for example, was a stone altar in the shape of a man, on which the still-beating hearts of the sacrificed victims were placed as offerings to the deities. In addition, the Tzompantli was a sort of rake on which the skulls of sacrificial victims and of enemies killed in battle were skewered for display. Finally, we should mention the sacred cenote, a large, natural well into which boys and girls were thrown to drown, to appease the gods.

In addition to the remains of large constructions with peristyle halls, among the best-known buildings are several large, pyramidal temples such as the so-called Castillo and the Temple of the Warriors. However, the Caracol temple offers the most interesting riddle of all: a round building, some scholars believe it was a temple to the god Kukulkan, while others think it was an astronomical observatory. Chichén Itzá's power waned after 1200 and Mayapán, the last bulwark of Maya civilization, took its place until it, too, declined.

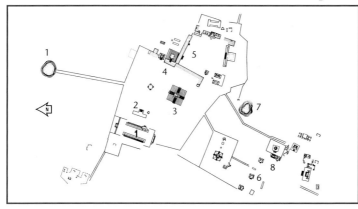

1) Ball court (Spheristerion)
2) Tzompantli
3) El Castillo
4) Temple of Warriors
5) Group of the Thousand
   Columns
6) Casa Colorada
7) Cenote
8) Caracol

UXMAL

At Uxmal also there are no inscriptions bearing dynastic genealogies. Some stone blocks bear engravings of the name of Chac, a ruler who is still mysterious.

At the close of the Classic age, many centers flourished in the Mexican peninsula of Yucatán; elsewhere, the Maya cities that had found their moments of glory in earlier centuries were moving toward a final state of decline and abandonment. Cities such as Uxmal, Labná, and Sayil began to flourish between 700 and 1000. Ruled by an uncultivated people, they nevertheless developed an elegant architectural style, called Puuc, after the name of the region in which they are located.

The city of Uxmal, situated in a magnificent natural landscape, contains some of the most amazing and refined examples of Puuc style. On this archaeological site rises the imposing Pyramid of the Magician (also known as House of the Magician and Pyramid of the Soothsayer), which was built on top of an oval base and consists of superimposed units. The name derives from a legend according to which the pyramid was built in one night by a sort of midget endowed with soothsaying powers, who had been challenged by a king.

The site's many buildings have a quadrangular base, typical of the region, with many rooms and interior courtyards, which sometimes are treated as squares due to their large size. Flanking the doors are porticoes with round columns, a style present only in this late phase of Maya art. The exterior walls are covered with mosaics consisting of millions of stone tesserae, whose unusual and geometric motifs recall weaving patterns.

The exterior of the House of the Nuns (also known as the Nunnery Quadrangle, so called by the first explorers because of the seventy-four small monastic-like cells comprising it) is decorated with large masks of Chac, the rain god, whose nose resembles an elephant's trunk. The main facade of the House of the Governor, which extends approximately three hundred feet (100 m), has mosaic-like decorations of geometric motifs suggestive of snakes, turtles, and human and divine beings. The overall iconographic effect and the elegant proportions place this palace among the jewels of Maya architecture. The main doors of the palace were built using the false vault, or corbel arch, technique. Due to the small number of epigraphic sources and the fact that—unlike other Maya cities—the genealogies of the ruling dynasties are missing, we still know very little about the history of Uxmal.

The Pyramid of the Magician is a large building resting on an oval base; it towers over the city of Uxmal and consists of several superimposed temples.

PACAL

Scholars named the most famous ruler of Palenque King Kin Pacal, or Sun Shield, because one of the glyphs used to refer to the king represents the stylized image of a shield.

In 1952, Mexican archaeologist Alberto Ruz discovered that below the Pyramid of the Inscriptions in Palenque, at a depth of about seventy-two feet (22 m), lay the funeral chamber of Lord Pacal (also known as Sun Lord Pacal and Hand Shield) who, before his death in A.D. 683 chose the prestigious temple as his tomb. Inside a large monolithic sarcophagus, the king's remains lay surrounded by precious jewels, among which were several jade fragments, which had originally been part of a funeral mask with eyes of mother of pearl and obsidian. An elegant stucco head, seventeen inches (43 cm) high, allows us to reconstruct Pacal's features.

On the surface of the large slab of stone that covered the sarcophagus was an engraved relief of a complex scene in which the deceased king is surrounded by a dense Maya cosmogony. The king stands next to the Tree of Life, or Cosmic Tree, which is one of the central elements of Maya religion, the axis connecting heaven to earth and the netherworld. A long inscription engraved along the border of the slab narrates the dates and the main events in the life of Pacal and his successors.

Kin Pacal, whose name means "Sun Shield," ascended the throne in 615 and ruled the city of Palenque until his death in 683. During this period, thanks to his political skills and deep artistic sensitivity, the city's ceremonial center grew to include prestigious buildings such as the Temple of the Inscriptions and the Palace. His son, Chan Bahlum (Snake Jaguar) who succeeded him, continued his father's work and built the Temple of the Sun, the Temple of the Cross, and the Temple of the Foliate Cross, which are rich in relief decorations.

In addition to the monumental architecture, the most precious testimony Pacal and his son left to posterity are the extremely long historical inscriptions, true dynastic lists, which date back to the year 431. The rich funeral appointments, which were meant to accompany the deceased Pacal in the realm of the netherworld, together with the inscriptions which speak of a close connection between the king and the mother goddess, indicate that the king was intent on increasing his prestige and political authority by claiming divine origin. Undoubtedly, King Kin Pacal is one of the more celebrated figures in the history of Classic-period Mayan cities.

This elegant stucco head found in King Pacal's burial chamber under the Temple of the Inscriptions is probably his portrait.

The features are refined and the king wears a regal headdress. Mexico City, Museo Nacional de Antropología.

SHIELD JAGUAR

LADY XOC

The inscriptions found on steles and lintels in Yaxchilán abundantly illustrate the accomplishments of Shield Jaguar, the king who beginning in 681 waged many wars and conquered many tribes, thus greatly expanding the boundaries of his kingdom.

Two stylized images of a shield and a jaguar make up the glyph that expresses the name of the famous king of Yaxchilán.

Several engravings portray the king in arms, in a position of superiority before subdued prisoners, or in ceremonial attire surrounded by dignitaries or family members. The capture of a feared enemy, the noble Ah Ahual, ruler of a still unidentified kingdom, was especially significant. The most interesting image, on Lintel 24, portrays the ruler next to his wife, who is ritually perforating her tongue with a thorn-studded rope to make it bleed. Shield Jaguar is holding a large torch, proof that this ritual took place behind closed doors or at night. Of note are the king's garments, which are those worn for important ceremonies and festivals.

Maya kings had at least one wife at their side. As evidenced by the glyphs, these women played an important, active role in court life and ceremonies. Even queen mothers were often portrayed next to their sons in iconographies and inscriptions. One special case is that of the city of Palenque, where during one historical period, succession to the throne was transmitted only to queens.

The inscriptions narrating the events of Yaxchilán's dynasties suggest that women such as Lady Xoc, wife of Shield Jaguar, played an important role in that city-state.

Lady Xoc of Yaxchilán, wife of Shield Jaguar, is represented on Lintel 24 engaged in an act of self-sacrifice to appease the gods. In Relief 25 she is shown alone, but here she is also richly clothed and bejeweled with a large jade necklace. The scene depicted in this second relief follows the preceding one. After losing blood from her self-inflicted wounds to the tongue, the queen apparently achieved a state of trance, in which the vision of the serpent appeared to her. According to Maya cosmogony, during ritual hallucinations a reptile of changing appearance appeared to the person in a state of trance and placed him or her in direct contact with the vision of a deity. In this case, Lady Xoc is contemplating the god Tlaloc, as he springs from the mouth of the snake in the guise of a warrior.

Wall panels from Yaxchilán, with relief decorations depicting Shield Jaguar and Lady Xoc performing self-mutilation, as a result of which they experienced hallucinations and made contact with the deities.

BIRD JAGUAR

After a power vacuum that lasted approximately ten years, caused by disputes about the legitimacy of the rulers, Bird Jaguar took the throne in October of

The stylized images of a bird and a jaguar appear in this glyph, which represents the name of another Yaxchilán ruler, son of Shield Jaguar.

747 and continued the territorial expansion his father, Shield Jaguar, had begun. He was responsible for the expansion of the city and for several architectural pieces. His accomplishments, like those of his predecessors, were celebrated in reliefs and inscriptions.

One such relief is quite interesting: it shows the newly enthroned young king playing ball, a ritual that was held right after his father's death to honor his memory before men and gods. The image of this king appeared often together with other female figures such as his mother, Lady Evening Star, who performed propitiatory rights jointly with him, and one of his wives, originally from another city, called Sky Lady, who offered him the royal robes and weapons before a battle.

In all probability, Bird Jaguar was the last important, charismatic king of Yaxchilán, because after his death no other memorial monuments were built, indicating a sudden political decline.

Left: *Yaxchilán relief of a dignitary.*
Right: *The Leiden Plate. Leiden, Rijksmuseum voor Volkenkunde.*

MOON ZERO BIRD

Among the most precious and celebrated finds is the Leiden Plate, an oval jade pendant eight and a half inches in length (22 cm), engraved on both sides. It was named after the Dutch

A bird, a zero, and the moon are the three elements of the name glyph of the mysterious Lord of Tikal, whose image appears on a small jade pendant known as the Leiden Plate.

city where it is preserved. Some scholars consider the plate to be a miniature stele, for one side bears the portrait of a king next to a prisoner bowing at his feet, while the other contains a complete inscription with chronological glyphs and a date indicating A.D. 320. Hence, the plate is slightly more recent than Stele 29 (dated 292), found in Tikal, the most ancient in Maya history.

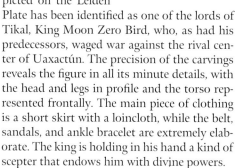

The individual depicted on the Leiden Plate has been identified as one of the lords of Tikal, King Moon Zero Bird, who, as had his predecessors, waged war against the rival center of Uaxactún. The precision of the carvings reveals the figure in all its minute details, with the head and legs in profile and the torso represented frontally. The main piece of clothing is a short skirt with a loincloth, while the belt, sandals, and ankle bracelet are extremely elaborate. The king is holding in his hand a kind of scepter that endows him with divine powers.

YAX PAC

Yax Pac, the six-teenth and last ruler of the reigning dynasty of Copán, was the son of King Smoking Shell, his predecessor, and a noble lady from Palenque. Yax Pac—

Yax Pac was the last ruler of the long-reigning dynasty of the city of Copán. The city's historical events are documented in numerous inscriptions.

whose name means "New Sun on the Horizon"—accorded great prominence to artists and scribes and greatly promoted culture, thus enriching the city with monuments and inscriptions. Soon after ascending the throne in 763, he skillfully tackled and solved a number of problems about agricultural production that had not kept up with the increase in population.

In later years, the king turned his interest to increasing the power and fame of his family. He began the restructuring of the ceremonial center adding new temples to the acropolis, among them Temple 11, with the monolithic altar referred to as Altar Q, with reliefs depicting all the representatives of his dynasty. Although it was Yax Pac's intention to create a lasting empire based on diplomacy and the cooperation of the elite, a few decades after his death in 820, the city of Copán entered a sudden decline.

YAX MOCH XOC

Yax Moch Xoc is considered the historic founder of the long-reigning dynasty of the city of Tikal. No monuments survive from the time in which he

This glyph expresses the name of a character who became almost mythical: the ancestor from whom the reigning dynasty of Tikal originated.

held power, however a memorial inscription dedicated to him composed a century and a half later allows us to date his ascent to the throne to A.D. 219. According to the inscription, his reign lasted thirty-nine years.

Yax Moch Xoc was certainly not the real founder of the dynasty, however he was so charismatic and his descendants worshiped him with such devotion that he came to be considered the real founder. The kings that came before him never enjoyed such fame, therefore they were not mentioned in the history of Tikal. Yax Moch Xoc was remembered in the inscriptions not only as a political leader, but also as a mythical ancestor, the originator of the noble stock that held sway over the state of Tikal.

Written texts have handed down to us more details about such other Tikal rulers as Smoking Frog and Noble Cacao.

King Yax Pac is shown together with the other fifteen rulers of Copán in a relief decorating the outside wall of Altar Q. The king, sumptuously dressed, is sitting cross-legged and wears a large headdress, probably decorated with feathers.

JAGUAR PAW

Seventy-three miles north of Tikal are the ruins of the ancient city of Calakmul. Although it is not one of the better known archaeological sites, in the Classic period Calakmul enjoyed a relative amount of political importance, as evidenced by the large number of memorial steles.

The two glyphs above refer to the name of a young king who in A.D. 686 ascended the throne of the city of Calakmul, a little-known Maya center whose ruins are seventy-three miles (120 km) from Tikal.

The inscriptions narrate that in April of A.D. 686 young Jaguar Paw took the throne of Calakmul. His crowning was a cause for celebration even beyond the political boundaries of Calakmul, especially in the nearby kingdoms of El Perú and Dos Pilas. For a long time, Calakmul and Dos Pilas enjoyed close links. Jaguar Paw had the honor of receiving the king of Dos Pilas—probably Flint Sky—as a guest to his coronation. In a scene painted on a vase, the young king kneels deferentially at the feet of Flint Sky. Perhaps the older king had taken on the role of godfather, which meant that a diplomatic alliance existed between the two kingdoms, thus maintaining an old-standing political arrangement between the two states.

Image taken from a vase painting of Jaguar Paw deferentially worshiping Flint Sky.

SMOKING FROG

One of the more challenging exploits of the rulers of Tikal was the capture of the city of Uaxactún—whose name in Maya means "eight stones"—located a few dozen miles to the south of Tikal. At the time of the military expedition, Tikal was under the rule of a powerful king known as Great Jaguar Paw. Nevertheless, the inscriptions in both cities give the name of a warrior, Smoking Frog, describing him as the true leader in the conquest of the city. He was undoubtedly a member of Tikal's nobility, because his name contains the emblematic glyph of that city.

Even today, Smoking Frog is the subject of scholarly debate: possibly a brother of Jaguar Paw, he became king of Uaxactún after capturing the city.

A reproduction, from 1959, of a wall painting from the city of Uaxactún, conquered by Commander Smoking Frog.

As a reward for the great valor shown as war leader, Smoking Frog received the throne of Uaxactún, which came under the permanent control of Tikal in the year 378. Attempts to reconstruct the genealogy of Smoking Frog have led some scholars to conclude that he was a brother of Great Jaguar Paw. In any case, this aristocratic commander ruled Uaxactún for many years, and continued to exert a charismatic role and powerful influence over the court of his native city.

NOBLE CACAO

CAUAC SKY

During the long reign of Noble Cacao (Ah Cacao), Tikal saw its greatest expansion as an urban center and the highest flourishing of its arts and architecture. His tomb, which was discovered in Palenque about ten years after that of Pacal, was, like Pacal's, buried beneath the main city temple, in a vaulted funeral chamber. His skeleton lay surrounded by semi-precious stones, pearls, shells, and jewelry, as well as precious accessories.

The name of one successor to Stormy Sky, who also contributed to the expansion of the city of Tikal, contains the glyph for cacao (or cocoa), *cacaw* in Maya.

Noble Cacao was peculiar for his age: he lived past the age of sixty and was five feet five inches (167 cm) tall. Ascending to the throne in May of 682, Noble Cacao immediately undertook to expand the ceremonial center, which up to then had been concentrated in the ancient northern acropolis. For this purpose, he surrounded himself with architects, craftsmen, and workers. It was his desire to transform the city of Tikal into a powerful metropolis that could rival neighboring kingdoms. Among the buildings we owe to him are Temple 1 and Temple 2, whose remains face the large central plaza, and which are among the most lavish expressions of Maya architecture.

Altar Q from Quiriguá, a monolithic monument. The relief shows a king or priest seated among the two heads of a two-headed monster, a recurring image in Maya iconography.

For a long time the small city of Quiriguá, located near the border of present-day Guatemala and Honduras, was under the control of powerful, nearby Copán. The time came however,

Cauac Sky, the most famous of Quiriguá's rulers, made life very difficult even for Eighteen Rabbit, the powerful king of Copán who became his prisoner.

when a king of this small city made life difficult for one of the most famous of Copán's rulers, Eighteen Rabbit. After a number of battles Cauac Sky succeeded in capturing Eighteen Rabbit and sacrificed him as a prisoner of war in the city square: the inscriptions found on Quiriguá's steles date this event to 738.

Cauac Sky's intent was to free his city, which from that time on acquired artistic prestige, but not to capture the city of Copán, whose territory, being too vast, would have been impossible to rule. The defeat, however, had a powerful effect on Copán, and it took many years for the city to regain the degree of power it had enjoyed under Eighteen Rabbit.

LORD

One ideographic-type glyph that was used to express the concept of "lord," *ahau* in Maya, represents a stylized vulture, its head girded by the band worn by the kings at the time of their coronation.

This glyph, translated into English as "lord," is one of the most important and recurring glyphs in Maya documents. The meaning is political rather than religious: he who holds absolute power, the king. Sometimes a more specific title was added to Lord: Mountain Lord, First Tree Lord, Sacred Sky Lord, and even Lord Cacao.

Based on epigraphic and archaeological data, most scholars now believe that the central political structure of Maya civilization was the monarchy. As the city-state's supreme authority, the king had divine power, similar to that of the Egyptian Pharaohs and the Peruvian Inca. Most of Maya architecture and art is a celebration of the monarch and his deeds, his conquests, and his military strategies.

In some cases, however, and this is especially true of Palenque, the king did not hold power alone but shared it with the lady—the queen-daughter or queen-wife—since in some cases women also inherited power. Recently decoded inscriptions yield a fairly complete picture of the history and deeds of many Maya lords. Many rulers left not only memorial monuments as proof of their magnificence, but rich funeral furnishings as well, thus ensuring that fame and wealth would accompany them on their last trip to Xibalbá, the kingdom of the dead.

There were different ways of writing the "lord" glyph: with a symbol indicating the day, with a human head, with a rodent, or using two phonetic forms.

This terra-cotta figurine shows a high-ranking official or a king, sumptuously dressed and bejeweled, sitting on a throne.

LADY

One glyph used to refer to the lady, the queen, *na* in Maya, is a face with feminine features. We have no detailed knowledge of women's role in Maya society, however written texts do indicate the existence of some illustrious queens.

W ritten inscriptions and reliefs tell the story of the ladies of the elite class—the mothers, daughters, and wives of kings—who were elegantly dressed and decorated with precious jewels. However, thanks to the reports of Spanish chroniclers, we also have some information about the life of the Maya women who belonged to the general population, although only with reference to Postclassic society.

Bartolomeo de las Casas and Diego de Landa described the role of women, especially as regards the marriage ritual. Unlike the aristocratic elite, men from the lower social classes were monogamous, though the least pretext sufficed to repudiate a wife, ask for a divorce, and immediately remarry. As with many other civilizations, marriages were arranged by the respective families and took place as soon as the young couple reached the appropriate age: for women, it was approximately the age of seventeen.

The wedding took place at the house of the bride's father. A priest opened the ceremony by burning incense and blessing the couple and, after a speech on marital duties, the banquet began. When the family could not afford the fee customarily collected by the priest, a wise village elder celebrated the marriage. One curious custom about the first wedding night was that one or more elderly women visited the couple at home to instruct them about sexual life, and left only after having made sure that everything had been clearly understood.

Many Jaina-style terracotta statuettes are of women, usually of refined ladies wearing jewels, headdresses, or elegant hairdos, probably court ladies or priestesses.
Above, left: *Art Museum of Princeton University.*
Left: *Museo Regional, Campeche.*

HE WAS DECORATED

The glyph expressing the sentence "He was decorated" was often used with reference to prisoners who had been captured in battle and decorated with special jewels and headdresses.

Stone reliefs, murals, and paintings on vases and bowls provide us with a fairly detailed idea of the clothes and ornaments worn by the nobility during festivals and civil and religious ceremonies. Amazing though it might seem, even the most powerful kings wore the loincloth, the principal piece of clothing for men. A narrow, very long cotton strip, it was wound several times around the waist and passed through the legs. Unlike the loincloths used by common men however, those worn by the kings had decorations of pearls and long, gaily colored feathers. The Aztec used a similar piece of clothing, called a *maxtlatl*.

On their shoulders kings wore an elegant embroidered cotton cape, the *patí*, also trimmed with precious feathers; sometimes they wore a jaguar skin instead of the cape. Common people also wore the *patí*, though in a smaller size and without trimmings. Major marks of distinction, even more important than clothing, were the scepters and headdresses, described later in this book, as well as pre-

cious jewels, which were reserved for the nobility. The more widely used jewelry were large necklaces, pectorals, bracelets, ankle bracelets, and ear pendants. Rings of all kinds were highly valued, including those for the nose and lips. The most popular materials were jade and obsidian, in addition to pearls, caiman teeth, and shells. The green feathers of the quetzal, a tropical bird that has been extinct for several centuries, were also highly valued, since the bird was held to be sacred.

As to gold and copper, we find wide documentation of its use only starting at the close of the Classic period. The reason for this is that unlike Peru's pre-Inca societies, the Maya regarded such semi-precious stones as jade as being more valuable than precious metals, which they did not know how to work.

Maya paintings and illustrations show dignitaries wearing long braided hair, sometimes wound around the head. They also painted their bodies with colors that had specific ritual meanings. As to footwear, by studying various reliefs and paintings scholars have been able to identify at least twelve types of leather sandals. The texts also describe the decorations of prisoners, since captured enemies were decked out with special types of ornamentation.

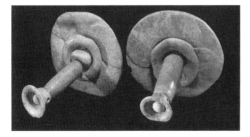

Above: *An elegantly dressed official, his hair arranged in a large braid.* **Left:** *Jade earrings and necklaces were among the favorite jewels of the Maya nobility. Denver, Denver Art Museum.*

HEADDRESS

The glyph expressing the word *headdress* recurs often in written texts, as every type of ritual required a specific head ornament. Like the scepter and jewelry, it was a symbol of royalty.

Relief sculptures, paintings on vases, and terra-cotta statuettes show several types of headdresses that were worn not just by the king but by all dignitaries, their wives, dancers, warriors, and the captured enemies who were fated to be sacrificed. There were headdresses for each specific occasion, and they took on special meanings depending on whether their use was for religious celebrations, sacrificial rites, marriage, or war. The portraits of several members of Copán's royal dynasty, carved on a stone altar, show each member wearing a different type of turban. Some of these headdresses were flat, others voluminous; they were usually decorated with ribbons and bird feathers.

One very popular headdress had a base of wicker or wood decorated with multi-colored parrot or quetzal bird feathers. Other populations of pre-Columbian America used similar headgear—a distinctive mark of social rank—for the same purposes. The Jaina-style statuettes constitute an unusually elegant and realistic aspect of Maya art, since they portray high-ranking men and women dressed in elaborate clothes and wearing bizarre headdresses, often conical or coiled.

In one mural at Bonampak, we see dignitaries in the act of humiliating prisoners who crouch at their feet. The dignitaries are portrayed wearing wooden animal heads of deer, jaguar, or fox, each one having a precise symbolic meaning. The choice of headdress depended on the specific type of ceremony: in this case, the submission of the vanquished. Shamans and priests also wore special headdresses, whose meanings were associated with the type of ritual they were celebrating.

A splendid Jaina-style terra-cotta figurine of a high-ranking dignitary, possibly a warrior, dressed in feathered attire and an imposing headdress. Jaina statuettes are particularly elegant and realistic examples of Maya art.

TO CAPTURE

This glyph expresses the verbs "to capture" and "to conquer," *bakwah* in Maya: two actions related to war and the taking of prisoners. The inscriptions narrate the kings' exploits in subduing the enemies.

Before scholars were able to decode the historical inscriptions engraved on stone monuments, a commonly held opinion characterized the Maya as a very peaceful people who spent their time studying the stars and building elegant public works, temples, and palaces. However, once the mysterious glyphs that tell of royal court events were decoded, such an opinion was no longer tenable. Hence, scholars were able to reconstruct, at least partially, the picture of a society that was extremely bellicose, even during the Classic age—and not only, as had been previously believed, after it came under Toltec domination.

The relief texts and images tell of continuing feuds among the many city-states and the different confederations, each one aiming to extend its territory and augment its political power. Kings are often pictured in military gear, armed with shields and spears, in the act of subduing war prisoners. The prisoners are shown crouching and in pain, their hands and feet bound, or with a rope tied around their neck, or being ferociously pulled by the hair.

Prisoners were fated to become slaves or sacrificial victims to one of the many gods. It was believed that shedding their blood would produce a bountiful harvest, thus ensuring the prosperity of the court and the wealth of the people. In fact, the god of war, whose image was painted black, was also associated with human sacrifice and was portrayed in the act of destroying homes by setting them on fire with a torch.

During the Postclassic period, under Toltec domination, war became a true obsession and a constant ritual for the Maya. During the Aztec period, endless bloody wars were fought, waged not to capture new territories, but prisoners, whose live hearts were then literally ripped from their chests and offered in sacrifice on stone altars called *chacmool*. We also note that battles and subjugations had to take place at specific times, as they were ruled by the position of the stars.

A Yaxchilán relief of Bird Jaguar standing before a kneeling prisoner. Probably captured in war, the man is shown with a rope around his neck and an unusual conical hat.

SHIELD

This glyph represents the stylized image of a shield, *pacal* in Maya. It appears in glyphs that express the names of several rulers, together with other words, such as Sun Shield and Shield Jaguar.

The shield glyph, coupled with such terms as "jaguar" and "sky," was a frequent element of the names of several kings. The shield is a recurrent image in Maya iconography, especially when kings are depicted as warriors or conquerors and armed with propelling weapons, flint-tipped spears, or pointed knives made of flint and obsidian.

American populations of the pre-Columbian age used several devices to battle the enemy, in addition to the shield. The Aztec used cotton-padded clothing, while the Maya protected the vulnerable parts of their bodies by wearing several wound layers of clothing. They covered their heads with a sort of helmet made of wood or metal.

Usually shields were round, but sometimes rectangular, and were made of wood, wicker, or leather. The more valuable shields usually had a surface decoration of vividly colored feathers from the quetzal or other tropical bird. Although there is no definite documentation, it is reasonable to believe that the Maya also decorated their wooden shields with lovely turquoise mosaics, as was the custom with the Mixtec people. Shields of this type were also part of the funeral furnishings of high-ranking Mixtec court dignitaries.

Terra-cotta figurine of a warrior dressed in battle gear and equipped with a round shield. Although this was the most popular shield shape, there were also rectangular shields, as can be seen from war scene iconography.

In the Aztec World

Although no Maya shields are extant, shields from other Mesoamerican civilizations have survived. At right is a magnificent, well-preserved example of an Aztec shield made with a mosaic of feathers decorated with gold thread. In the red background is a coyote. The shield probably belonged to King Ahuitzotl. Vienna, Ethnographic Museum.

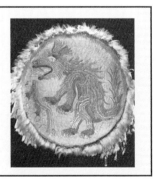

BIRTH

The name of the glyph most frequently used to refer to birth was "standing frog" because of its shape. The Maya word most often used to express the concept of birth was *sih*.

Birth, like death or any human event, was not considered to be a casual occurrence, since it was fraught with religious meaning and unequivocally connected to the calendrical cycle and position of the stars, from which everything depended. The inscriptions reported in great detail the date of birth of each prince and the names of his parents, stressing their importance for the newborn's future political role. In the case of polygamous kings with foreign wives, the newborn was expected to strengthen alliances and diplomatic treaties. Thus, each newborn was precisely located within the framework of the whole royal lineage and his various relations, including siblings and stepsiblings. The newborn's titles of nobility were also included in the inscriptions.

There were ceremonies at court both before and after birth. From Diego de Landa we learn that the common people also performed them. When the contractions came, a priestess would celebrate propitiatory rites to Ix Chel, the goddess of fertility. After the birth, all the delivery tools, such as the hot stone that had been placed on the mother's womb to ease her pain, were thrown into a spring together with offerings to the gods. The baby also received a sort of purifying baptism. The umbilical cord was cut on a day prescribed by the stars, using a knife set into a corncob. The cob was then shelled and buried during the sowing season, that the kernels might nourish the child, bringing it strength and prosperity.

We have scant information regarding the education of Maya children, except for some reports by Diego de Landa. Presumably, instruction was strictly for the elite, and only high-ranking boys could to attend school. The situation was quite different in the Aztec world, whose chroniclers have left us detailed information. In the Aztec capital of Tenochtitlan, in addition to the temple schools attended by aristocratic boys and girls, there were also several public schools. All parents, even those of poor social standing, were required to enroll their children, beginning at the age of fifteen, so that they might become good subjects, dancers, and warriors.

These appealing statuettes of a mother and child from Kaminaljuyú probably date to the earliest phase of Maya civilization. Guatemala City, Museo de Arqueología y Etnografía.

ASCENT TO POWER

Several glyphs were used to express the ascent to the throne. The two glyphs pictured to the left translate the expression "The band was wound around his head." This ritual took place during the coronation.

Glyphs with different meanings expressed the crowning ceremony, an important part of life at court. Specific celebrations and rituals such as sacrifices, the taking of hallucinogenic substances, and the burning of incense by priests always surrounded this event.

The most frequently recurring and meaningful glyph refers to the ritual of winding a royal band around the king's head. Some texts described it thus: "He knotted the band" or "He took his seat wearing the band," or " The band was knotted for him." Usually, the white color of the headband was stressed. Together with the scepter, the band decorating the king's head was one of the noblest symbols of royalty, removed only at his death.

Another expression referred to the king's ascent to power by using the verb "to present": "He was presented," with the glyph clearly showing a hand extended in the corresponding act. Other glyphs expressed the actual ascent to the throne: "He sat" or "He was placed on the throne." Several small terra-cotta throne models have survived. A less frequent, though still meaningful, version is the glyph that translates the term "exit." According to reliable interpretations, the word referred to the moment when the king came out of the temple at the conclusion of the ceremony in which the priests had consecrated him and his position.

The epigraphic texts have handed down to us precise dates corresponding to the ascent to the throne of many kings. As with all other important events, the choice of the coronation day was not casual, but was taken after prolonged study of the calendar and position of the stars.

Terra-cotta figurine of a high-ranking official seated on a throne supported by jaguars. The dress and countenance indicate a solemn moment. Many miniature thrones have been found, often with the jaguar as decorative motif. Mexico City, Kurt Stavenhagen Collection.

DEDICATION

Usually, words indicating a dedication are followed by the name of the object or the monument being dedicated. The inscriptions tell of the many dedication ceremonies the kings performed on special occasions.

Palenque's Temple of the Sun, one of three temples built by King Chan Bahlum, son of Pacal, between A.D. 683 and 692. Inscriptions narrate how the temple's dedication ceremony coincided with a precise astral phenomenon.

Several verbs expressed the act of dedicating something to someone. In the inscriptions, the specific glyph expressing this verb was usually followed by a glyph identifying the subject matter of the dedication and the name of the person or deity to whom it was made.

Scholars have noted that for the most part the dedications referred to buildings, parts of buildings, monuments, or votive shrines. Only rarely were other types of objects dedicated.

Usually, inscriptions reported the precise details of the dedication such as the king, the queen, or the god to whom the dedication was made; the exact date; and, often, the circumstances that had led to the occasion. The kings regularly dedicated to themselves and to other family members large memorial steles, public buildings, and ball courts. Large pyramids surmounted by temples, sacrificial altars, and religious statues, were dedicated to the gods, particularly during various festivals marking calendrical cycles and astronomical phenomena. For example, Palenque's inscriptions report that King Chan Bahlum celebrated the dedication of the Temples of the Cross precisely on the date of the alignment of the planets Jupiter and Saturn.

DECAPITATION

This is a phonetic glyph consisting of three syllables composing the word *chu ah ka* which means "decapitation." The term recurred frequently in historical texts.

Decapitation was practiced not just by the Maya, but by almost all the populations of pre-Columbian America. This cruel and gruesome act, in addition to being a sign of victory or a form of extreme punishment, was imbued with a profound ritual meaning.

In Peru, the iconography of the Nazca people in particular emphasizes the importance of trophy heads. These were the dried hollow skulls of enemies that warriors hung as decoration from their belts and clothes, or placed in warriors' tombs as genuine war trophies. In the Mesoamerican regions, the ritual of decapitating prisoners of war was, first of all, a way of propitiating the gods: the blood being shed would feed the earth, fertilizing it. The same fate applied to the players who were sacrificed after the ball game. There is sound evidence that this macabre tradition, connected to the most popular ritual game of the Maya and the Aztec, had its roots in Olmec culture.

The Tzompantli of Chichén Itzá is evidence of how, in the Postclassic period especially, decapitation had become an obsession, for the stone frieze of carved skulls reproduced a real wooden palisade on which the heads of the sacrificed victims were impaled and displayed.

Chichén Iztzá's Tzompantli is a Toltec stone monument reproducing the actual wooden stake fence on which the heads of dead enemies and sacrificial victims were displayed.

SACRIFICE

This glyph is phonetic, consisting of the syllables *na wa ha,* and has several meanings: "sacrifice," "dress," and "marriage." Often the concept of sacrifice was expressed by referring to the dress appropriate for the occasion.

The concept of sacrifice, understood as a propitiatory act to placate or befriend the gods, is a fundamental element of the spiritual and religious world of the Maya. The Aztec, the Inca, and all the other less known populations of pre-Columbian America also shared this concept. The sacrifice of human beings and jaguars, deer, and turkeys was intrinsic to all kinds of ceremonies—births, marriages, royal coronations, and wars—in addition to the celebrations of the calendar cycle. Even dances and the ritual ball game ended with a sacrifice. Shedding blood was an indispensable way of placating the gods—whose wrath was manifested by recurring famines and droughts—or simply a way of pleasing them, of nourishing the soil, or a means of obtaining the favors of all the cosmic forces.

Archaeological evidence and the descriptions of Spanish chroniclers lead us to under-stand that this cruel ritual had become an al-most daily occurrence in the Postclassic peri-od. In fact, according to the Toltec and Aztec tradition, it was imperative that the rain god Chac-Tlaloc and the Kukulkan-Quetzalcoatl god be nourished incessantly.

In the most common ritual, the victim was forced to lie on a stone altar, the *chacmool,* after being coated with blue, the sacrificial color. Then, using sharp flint knives, the priests in charge of the ritual extracted the still-beating heart from the victim's chest and offered it to the deities. Several reliefs and wall paintings from Chichén Itzá show this blood-curdling sacrifice in detail.

Moreover, to ensure the favor of the rain god, human beings of all ages and of both sex-es were periodically thrown into the cenote, a sacred well. To make the sacrifice even more pleasing to the gods, incense, pottery, and jew-elry were also thrown into the well.

The chacmool, *a mono-lithic altar in the shape of a reclining man, was used beginning in the Postclas-sic period for a unique, macabre and dreadful sacrifice: the extraction by four priests of the still-beating hearts of human victims. Mérida, Museo Regional de Antropología de Yucatán.*

SELF-SACRIFICE

These two glyphs are ideographic, and express the concept of "self-sacrifice." The glyph on the left shows an obsidian lancet used for this purpose, while the second glyph shows a hand pouring blood or incense.

In addition to sacrificing human beings and animals in rituals that entailed atrocious suffering followed by death, the Maya also practiced self-sacrifice. Two glyphs in particular indicate this action: one of them literally means "bloodletting." Self-sacrifice (or self-mutilation) was practiced only by the religious  and political elite. Several texts illustrated by reliefs narrate that in situations requiring sacrifices, kings and queens would cause their own blood to be shed while in a state of deep stupor induced by incense, wild dances, and drugs.

For men, the ritual consisted in piercing their penis with sharp obsidian lancets or with thorns, and threading the perforations with thin straws; women did the same on their tongue or lips. The blood shed by specific body parts, the genital organs in particular, was believed to nourish the earth, thus promoting fertility and a bountiful maize harvest.

During the self-sacrifice ritual the king or queen would fall into a state of trance and experience hallucinations. They would see the vision of the sacred serpent, which was the symbol of the blood being shed. According to Maya cosmology, the vision was the way by which mortals could make contact with the heavens or with the underground world of Xibalbá.

Thus, gods as well as ancestors were called down to earth during the act of self-mutilation and could speak and foretell the future. There is no doubt that the snake, usually represented as a feathered dragon, was one of the major symbols of Maya cosmology.

Right: *A Jaina-style figurine of a significant example of self-mutilation: here a man dressed in ceremonial headdress pierces his penis with a pointed tool—an obsidian knife or thorn—to cause blood to flow.*
Above: *drawing after a glyph expressing the concept of self-mutilation.*

APPEAR, MANIFEST

These two glyphs are a literal translation of "to manifest" and "to appear," and refer to specific occasions when individuals reached states of trance with hallucinatory visions, which were believed to be supernatural manifestations.

In addition to self-sacrifice, there were other ritual methods that allowed kings and priests to reach the state of trance that induced visions and supernatural manifestations, which in turn brought them in contact with the world of the gods. While loss of blood was the most common method, it was not the only one: the Maya were acquainted with several substances that, when ingested, altered the senses and produced hallucinatory states.

Since at least Olmec times, these practices had also spread to other Mesoamerican peoples. Among the popular substances were, first of all, fermented drinks, such as those made with agave and maize. According to the Spanish chroniclers, the most common of these was *balché* mead, produced by mixing fermented honey with the bark of a tree of the *Lonchocarpus* genus.

The best narcotic plant, however, was wild tobacco *(Nicotiana rustica):* men used to roll up the leaves into large cigars, as depicted in several interesting vase paintings. Smoking these cigars led to a true state of trance, since wild tobacco is much stronger than today's cultivated species. Several rituals, the shamanistic ones in particular, included the use of hallucinogenic mushrooms. These were mountain mushrooms with a high level of narcotic substances. The Maya gave different names to each kind of mushroom, depending on the type of vision or hallucination it produced after ingestion. Even today, shamans eat these hallucinogenic mushrooms in the course of specific rituals, enabling them to have a large number of visions that connect them to the supernatural world.

Several reliefs and vase paintings show that the fermented alcoholic drinks were introduced in the body also by means of enemas, since absorption of these substances through the intestine is faster and produces a quicker effect. The Spanish chroniclers reported the use of other narcotic plants as well, however this has not been confirmed by archaeological findings. Among these was the water lily, whose narcotic effect was believed to approach that of the lotus flower.

Vase painting of a man smoking a cigar. Cigars of wild tobacco were much stronger than today's cigars made of cultivated tobacco.

BLOOD

Several glyphs and symbols express "blood." The most common is a sort of cylindrical roll, with pearl-encrusted borders, inside which are visible the jade and shell glyphs.

According to Maya religion, life depended most on blood. Together with the flow of water, the flow of this lymph symbolized the flow of the universe, the balance between spirit and matter, and was the key for accessing the Godhead.

One unusual element of this civilization was the number of rituals that were intended to cause blood to flow from the bodies of prisoners of war. In other rituals, shamans and rulers inflicted the same procedure on themselves. Using sharp, pointed obsidian lancets, they made blood pour from their own bodies, especially precious blood from the genitals. After reaching a state of deep stupor induced by burning incense and ingesting drugs, the ritual culminated in the bloodletting. Each drop being shed would nourish the gods and the earth, ensuring a new, abundant maize harvest that would feed the people and provide wealth for the court.

Blood was represented by many iconographic elements. The most complex of these was a monstrous, dragon-like creature with a marked nose and a pearl-encrusted mouth, usually shown issuing from the Cosmic Tree. The most common symbol, however, was a cylindrical roll with pearl-encrusted borders, inside which the glyphs of the red, yellow, and blue were visible, or the glyphs of such precious materials as jade, shell, and bone.

Each of these images stressed the precious nature of blood and its link to such life-generating elements as water, which was represented by a green semi-precious stone. The simple glyph reproduced above is a stylized image of blood gushing from one of these precious elements.

Several tools were used for bloodletting, especially for self-mutilation.
Far left: *a ceremonial flint lancet from Lamanai, Belize.*
Left: *a sharp stingray spine. Thorns from agave and similar plants were also used to pierce sensitive body parts, as shown in the Yaxchilán relief of Lady Xoc piercing her tongue with a sharp thorn-threaded cord.*

FLINT

The glyph representing flint, *tok* in Maya, shows a stylized artifact, a cutting tool made of this stone. Like obsidian, it was used for self-mutilation.

The Maya were in the habit of setting up hiding places in which to store offerings to the gods or the deceased. Such offerings always included precious objects that had a ritual meaning. The hiding places for the gods were dug under temples at the time of the dedication ceremony; in those for the dead, the offerings were placed inside tombs as part of the funeral furnishings. Additionally, archaeologists have discovered hiding places under steles and altars, and near the walls of residential complexes.

These secret storage spaces contained for the most part jade, shell, and mother-of-pearl jewelry, together with fine pointed tips made of stingray spines and special flint or obsidian blades and objects. These two stones were the hard stones of the Maya, who had no metal tools. They used them as tips for spears, as knives, and as blades for farm work. The Maya believed flint had been created by the rain and storm gods and sent to earth in the form of lightning. Thus, over time, this stone had acquired supernatural powers and significance.

Toward the end of the Classic period, craftsmen began to use flint to fashion precious and unusual objects with human, divine, and animal shapes: they are the so-called "eccentric flints," and they were originally used as ceremonial scepters. This is a refined, unusual aspect of Maya art.

Flint and obsidian are also mentioned in Postclassic Maya sacred texts, and here also these stones were imbued with a cosmogonic meaning.

An unusual carved piece of flint. This stone was carved into unusual human or animal shapes and were used for ritual purposes and as scepters during ceremonies. Cleveland, Cleveland Museum of Art.

SAGE

These glyphs refer to a class of educated people active in the arts and sciences, such as sculptors and scribes, who played an important role at court.

These glyphs were assigned a generic meaning, which was made specific by the context in which they were used. The first meaning is that of "sage," a court official, someone who is educated and possesses knowledge or someone who acts wisely, respecting the will of the gods and obeying the ruler.

The second meaning is that of "artist." Schools of architects and craftsmen, considered true artists by the rulers, worked at the Maya royal courts. They were for the most part sculptors, always busy making stone monuments decorated with stuccoes and reliefs; painters who decorated the walls of palaces and temples with lively scenes and colors such as, for example, the well-preserved frescoes of the rooms of Bonampak's acropolis; pottery makers, goldsmiths, and weavers. The scribes were another class of artists. A restricted caste that enjoyed great consideration among the commoners—for whom learning to write was forbidden—they held great privileges with the kings of the Classic age, who employed them to transmit to their descendants their glorious deeds.

Another meaning assigned to these glyphs is "scientist." For the Maya, the scientists were probably sages who studied and interpreted the heavenly phenomena and knew the calendrical cycles that were closely linked to the gods, and on which all of life's events depended. Many of these scientists wrote astrological almanacs and astronomical treatises on agave-leaf codices, of which only four examples have survived. Among the scientists were also healers, physicians, and shamans. The figure of the shaman is very ancient, and certainly predates

Statue of the guardian god of scribes, from Copán. Sometimes this deity is shown with monkey or rabbit features. Like astronomers, scribes were a privileged and highly valued caste, their knowledge restricted only to the few initiates, not the general population.

Olmec civilization. It was the shaman's role to contact the gods through special rituals. Each shaman possessed an animal alter ego, called *uay* by the Maya and *nahual* by the Aztec: the jaguar was considered the most important *nahual*.

MIDGET

This glyph was used to indicate a class of people who were part of the ruler's entourage: the midgets. They filled the role of servants and enjoyed great respect.

The Spanish conquistadors who came into contact with Aztec court life noticed that among the throng of aristocrats, servants, and slaves who surrounded the ruler, were several midgets, who were treated with great respect—almost veneration.

The same was probably true of Maya royal houses. In fact, the paintings on vases and walls depict extremely short people, elegantly dressed, standing next to the ruler, just like any other gentlemen at court. The iconography of other cultures, such as the Peruvian Mochica, also show midgets as a recurring theme, as if they enjoyed particular importance in their society.

In the Maya, Aztec, and Peruvian societies, the same was true of deformed individuals—such as the lame and, especially, hunchbacks. The reports of the Spanish chroniclers narrate that these physical anomalies were treated as divine manifestations: it was believed that their small, deformed bodies housed a god; for this reason they enjoyed great respect. Thus, instead of being despised, these individuals were held in high consideration. Statuettes representing small, crippled human beings were found in Olmec archaeological strata, leading us to believe that this attitude had very ancient origins. An analogous example, in Europe, was that of the Gonzaga, a noble Italian Renaissance family who kept a whole family of midgets at their court.

This charming vase painting shows a dignitary surrounded by a retinue of servants. A very small man, identified as a midget, offers a mirror to his lord.

DEATH

Among the many glyphs expressing the concept of death, the one on the left is an exact translation of "to die," "to extinguish oneself": *ch'a yi* in Maya.

The Maya language used several different glyphs to express the concept of death and the verb to die. Some of them translated the act of passing literally: "to expire," "to extinguish oneself," "to end."

One alternative expression meant "to untie the head-girding band." This expression referred to the ritual act of removing from the deceased king the ornaments of power he had received at his coronation, of which the white band was the most important.

Different groups of symbols also described death as a time of passage from a physical to a spiritual state: "He [the king] took the road of Xibalbá"; "He exhaled his white flower." The first sentence refers to the deceased's journey to the Maya afterlife. The second is a poetic rendering of the concept according to which the soul was compared to a white flower, blown out of the body along with the last sigh of life.

Understandably, the ruler's death was surrounded by ceremonies and sacrifices intended to make his journey to the netherworld more comfortable and peaceful. For until he arrived at Xibalbá, his spirit would be exposed to good and evil cosmic forces, and this meant a danger for the entire population, who anxiously waited for a new ruler to ascend the throne.

There is a large body of research on the significance of Xibalbá, a realm described in *Popol Vuh* and portrayed in many vase and wall paintings. The name derives from "Xib," a word expressing the concept of terror or fear. According to *Popol Vuh*, it was a fearful place, peopled by monstrous beings and negative forces, which the soul had to pass through on

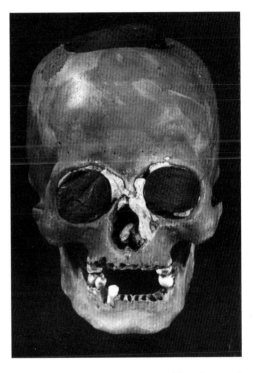

This dreadful symbol of death is an incense burner made from a skull. It was recovered from the sacred well at Chichén Itzá.

a sort of purification course before it could reincarnate on earth. According to other descriptions from the Classic period, however, Xibalbá was not such a cruel place, but rather a world of lakes and rivers, with clear cosmogonic references to water and its deities.

BURIAL

This glyph which refers to the burial of a deceased person, is phonetic, being composed of the syllables *mu ka ah*. In Maya it means "to have been buried" or "to be hidden underground."

Diego de Landa provided an interesting description of Maya Postclassic funeral customs. According to his eyewitness account, the common people buried their dead under the floor of their huts, or close by. The body was wrapped in a shroud, and small jade pearls or kernels of maize were placed in the mouth of the deceased to nourish him during the journey to the afterlife or as an offering to ease his access to the kingdom of the dead.

Among the nobility however, cremation was common. The urn containing the ashes was buried and a religious building was erected on the site. Archaeological finds in Chichén Itzá and other sites confirm this custom. It is, however, a late tradition, in all probability introduced by the Toltec, because from the dawn of Maya civilization up to the end of the Classic period, the only known funeral rite was burial.

Hidden under the pyramids of several temples archaeologists have uncovered the rich tombs of rulers, for example of Pacal in Palenque and Eighteen Rabbit in Copán, along with the tombs of nobles and priests. They were filled with all kinds of jewels, weapons, and precious objects that were meant to ease

the deceased's last journey and ensure them every kind of comfort in the afterlife.

In Oaxaca, the Postclassic Mixtec of Monte Albán buried their notables "escorted" by their dogs and their slaves, whom they sacrificed for this purpose.

Many tribes of pre-Columbian America followed practically identical customs: on the southern coast of Peru, in the tombs of the Paracas-Nazca people, archaeologists have found bodies that had been buried wrapped in long, decorated shrouds. They were preserved intact thanks to the dry climate. In the northern part of Peru, a recently excavated tomb of a Moche-period notable revealed that he had been buried with his enormous wealth and a number of slaves and concubines. From the magnificence of his tomb it is safe to believe that this deceased dignitary—whom archaeologists have called Lord of Sipan—had occupied a prestigious office, comparable in all respects to that of the Maya kings.

A precious jade mask, part of the funerary objects belonging to Palenque's King Pacal. The eyes are made of mother of pearl and obsidian; a T-shaped amulet found in the mouth is evidence the deceased had taken on a divine role. Mexico City, Museo Nacional de Antropología.

SYMBOLS

The cardinal points, the colors, and
the numbers were the key to the knowledge
of the universe, the stars, and time. Maya sacred
scriptures reveal the importance and esoteric
function of numbers, the link between cardinal
points and colors, each one imbued with
a deep religious significance.

CARDINAL POINTS AND NUMBERS

Proof of the extremely advanced level reached by Maya culture is given by their astonishing mathematical and astronomical knowledge.

The study of arithmetic was not an end in self, for each number had a precise spiritual content and was linked to a specific time of the year, a historical event, and a particular deity. All of Maya cosmogony was permeated with the symbolic meaning of numbers, all of them inevitably linked to each other. This conception had its roots in ancient Olmec and Zapotec cultural matrices, which the Maya developed and perfected.

In the field of mathematics, the Maya were probably the first to use the concept of zero. This important intellectual discovery that allowed them to organize their vigesimal numeration in a positional system, establishing the number twenty as a unit of progression. They never used the European decimal (base ten) system, which was also used in other parts of the world.

Usually, numbers were arrayed in columns and read from the bottom to the top, or, if they were set horizontally, they were read from the right to the left. Computing was done by multiplying each higher-order number by the number twenty, to obtain lower-order numbers.

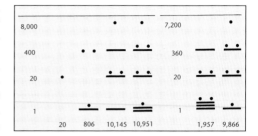

A table with examples of Mayan positional mathematics. The vigesimal computation, based on twenty (unlike the Western decimal metric system, which is based on ten) is shown in the col- umn at left and is read from bottom to top. The number twenty is shown by one dot in the second column. On the right is the chronological computation used to record calendrical cycles.

Like words, numbers could be expressed by different signs: the simplest method was the use of dots for units and bars for the number five. Thus, combinations of bars and dots expressed the numbers from one to nineteen. Twenty was expressed by the moon glyph. According to the context, zero was expressed by the shell glyph or a stylized flower. Often, in the texts, dot-and-bar numbers were replaced by the heads of

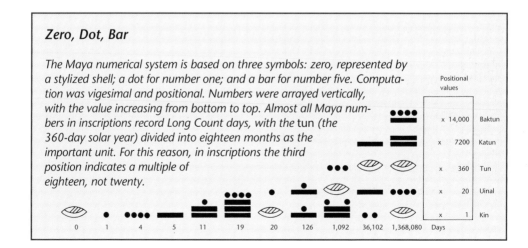

Zero, Dot, Bar

The Maya numerical system is based on three symbols: zero, represented by a stylized shell; a dot for number one; and a bar for number five. Computation was vigesimal and positional. Numbers were arrayed vertically, with the value increasing from bottom to top. Almost all Maya numbers in inscriptions record Long Count days, with the tun (the 360-day solar year) divided into eighteen months as the important unit. For this reason, in inscriptions the third position indicates a multiple of eighteen, not twenty.

	Positional values	
x 14,000		Baktun
x 7200		Katun
x 360		Tun
x 20		Uinal
x 1		Kin

| 0 | 1 | 4 | 5 | 11 | 19 | 20 | 126 | 1,092 | 36,102 | 1,368,080 | Days |

deities—called "portrait (or head) variants"—associated with each number, which in turn could be replaced by a whole figure.

Diego de Landa recounts that even in the sixteenth century, Maya merchants used to do their bookkeeping using the ancient computing system on a sort of simple abacus, improvised with cocoa beans.

Mathematical computations were the foundation of astronomical studies, calendrical cycles, and religious rites. Narratives of all royal events always included the dates of occurrence. This rigid, exact narrative system has enabled scholars to date with accuracy much of the history of the Maya reigning houses. An exclusive caste of educated priests was in charge of studying numbers and making complex astronomical computations.

The four codices and sacred texts, including the *Popol Vuh*, on the other hand, illustrate the important role of numbers in religion and cosmogony. The sole creator god, Hunab Ku, had begotten four children, named Bacab, and had placed four cardinal points at the four corners of the world to support it. At the center was the Cosmic Tree—appropriately called the World Tree—that acted as a link between the sky, the earth, and the netherworld. The four brothers were represented as ceiba trees and each one of them, as well as the center, had a stone and a color associated with them.

Maya and Arabic numbering

This table has another example of the vigesimal, positional Maya numerical system, compared to the Arabic numerical system adopted in Europe.

Position	Value	Maya numbers	Arabic numbers
4a.	8,000	(3)	24,000
3a.	400	(8)	3,200
2a.	20	(2)	40
1a.	1	(5)	5

The Aztec and other Mesoamerican peoples had very similar beliefs about the creation and the structure of the universe, possibly derived from common ancestral matrices.

The cardinal points, the colors, and the numbers, considered equivalent to deities, permeated all of Maya history and religion. There were innumerable links and references between them, the heavenly gods, the stars, and all the calendrical cycles. Symbolic numbers such as two, four, thirteen, and multiples of three recur periodically in the astronomical almanacs and clearly had a major role not only in religion but also in everyday life.

This knowledge and these conceptions, based as they were on the belief that calculation was fundamental, continue to astonish scholars to this day. The Maya probably perfected systems that had their origin in Olmec and Zapotec culture, which they brought to an exceptionally advanced level—only a small part of which has come down to us.

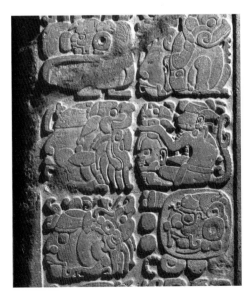

Glyphs on the limestone relief of Lintel 48 from Yaxchilán, dated to A.D. 524. The inscription contains a Long Count calendrical computation. Interestingly, numbers are not expressed with dots and bars, but with portraits, probably of deities whose identity is unknown. Mexico City, Museo Nacional de Antropología.

EAST—RED

The glyph for the cardinal point east, *lakin* in Maya, is combined with the glyph of the rising sun's color. The east was identified with the planet Venus and the color red.

The Maya classified east as the main direction, since it was that of the rising sun. The term expressing this cardinal point changed according to the various languages and to whether the speaker was looking toward east or had his back to it: "strong sun," "born sun," "arrived sun," and "next sun." The concept of the Orient was symbolically associated with the sun god and with life, in antithesis to west, which was the direction of war and death. In astronomy, east was identified with the planet Venus, as the Morning Star.

Red, the color associated with this cardinal point, had numerous references: the sun, blood, fire, the sap of the sacred ceiba tree, and roasted corn. All these symbols expressed vital force. Blood—which the Maya believed was a divine element—was abundantly shed during sacrifices and self-mutilations, for it was believed it would nourish the earth and the gods.

Based on historical and archaeological sources, following the arrival of the Toltec in the Postclassic period, bloodletting became increasingly more important, with a concurrent rise in sacrificial cults. During the last phase of the Aztec empire, a gruesome custom was introduced, that of the Flower Wars. Unlike other wars, these were not waged for territorial expansion, but to capture increasingly larger numbers of human victims whose blood would go to nourish the cruel tribal god Huitzilopochtli.

As for Maya beliefs, even the water that flowed in the river of the netherworld, the Xibalbá, was full of blood. The ceiba tree was believed to be sacred because its branches shed a red lymph, for which reason it was likened to the mythical Cosmic Tree.

Because of its many symbolic meanings and its brightness, the color red was held in high esteem and appears often in codices, in wall decorations and pottery. A mineral pigment was used to produce it, while a purple dye produced by a sea mollusk was used to color precious cotton textiles. Finally, the flame-red feathers of tropical birds such as the hummingbird and the Ara macaw decorated the dresses of noble dignitaries.

Cylinder vase from Piedras Negras. Red, one of more popular colors for painting, was connected to the concepts of life and the rising sun; it was also the color of the ceiba tree's sap and symbolic of the Cosmic Tree.

WEST—BLACK

The west glyph, in *chikin* Maya, is here combined with the glyphs of its corresponding color, black (*ek* in Maya), related to death. The west was believed to represent death.

While east was the place of life and the rising sun, the west represented death, war and, like ancient cultures all over the world, the kingdom of the dead. Some definitions of the west were "the eaten sun," "the underground sun," "the departed sun," all synonyms of darkness.

The night sun was contrasted with the sun god, guardian of light and life. The former was embodied in the jaguar, which represented the sun during its invisible nightly transit in the bowels of the earth, unseen by men.

In the codices, the deities of death and of war, as well as Ix Tab, the goddess of suicide, were depicted with traces of dark paint around the body and the eyes. In fact, the color black (coal was used in paintings to render this color) was associated with the west and death.

For the Maya, the darkness of the night, of the deep caves that ran along the mountain slopes, and of the murky waters of the cenote, the sacred sacrificial well, was the path through which men could approach the gods. Many geographical names in Maya inscriptions refer to places with "black wells" or "black holes," a clear reference to naturally formed water wells. Kings and shamans held hallucinatory rites and self-sacrifices in the dark of night and in caves lit only by torchlight. The sacrificial victims who managed not to drown after being thrown into the cenote received the gifts of prophecy and divination. Black was also the color of obsidian, the shining black rock of volcanic origin which the Maya believed had been created by lightning. Unlike the Maya, the Aztec used the color white to represent the west, to which Quetzalcoatl was assigned, and called it "the women's place."

Obsidian, a volcanic rock, was used to make tools and the small, symbolic figures shown here. The Maya believed obsidian was created by lightning.

SOUTH—YELLOW

The south glyph, *nohol,* is shown at left together with the glyphs for the color yellow, *kan,* symbolizing the sun and maize. For the Aztec, the south was associated with blue.

In Yucatec the south was *nolh,* and in Cholti it was *nohol:* both expressed the concept of "the sun's large side" or "the sun's right side." Unlike contemporary cartographic convention, for the Maya the uppermost part of the universe was east, and south was to its right.

Yellow was the color associated with south: in antiquity, as well as today, it symbolically recalled the sun, ripe ears of corn, and even the background color of the jaguar's spotted skin, all major symbols of strength and life.

On the other hand, for the Aztec, the color blue was the one associated with the south, and Huitzilopochtli, the tribal god of sun and war and of Tenochtitlan, was its guardian. In art, we find yellow in some murals, such as those that decorate the royal tombs of Bonampak. As with the color red, the pigment to reproduce yellow was extracted from oxidizing mineral powders.

These Bonampak frescoes, together with others from the Classic period, depict warriors and kings with headdresses and ornaments of yellow feathers, for the most part from the Ara macaw and yellow-blue Ara parrot (*Ara ararauna*).

Here we should say a few words about these three major elements of Maya culture, even though they will be covered in later chapters. Maize was the primary agricultural crop in all of Mesoamerica, and the basic food staple. The maize plant was protected by its own deity, and both the plant and the god were represented by the same glyph. The sun and the rain had a special role in the ripening of maize, and in the abundance and quality of the harvest. Thus countless rites took place to ensure that maize fields received adequate nourishment: kings and priests shed their blood in self-mutilation rituals in order to nourish the earth and fertilize it. Maize, and the sun that made it grow, thus signified abundance and life. The animal that best represented this concept was the jaguar, the most important divine double, symbol of the sun in its nightly journey.

Detail of wall painting in Room 2, Structure 1 at Bonampak. The richly decorated room is painted in vivid colors, yellow especially. Maya kings liked to wear headdresses made of yellow feathers from the Ara macaw and the yellow-blue Ara parrots.

NORTH—WHITE

North, *xaman* in Maya, was associated with the color white, *sak*, symbol of royalty and purity. north was the farthest cardinal point, where the North Star, guide of the merchants, resided.

For the Maya people and other inhabitants of tropical lands, north was the most distant cardinal point. They referred to it as "the sun's left side" or "the place next to paradise." The North Star, an important star around which the celestial sphere revolved, had its mysterious abode in the north, and from the north each year came the cold winter rains that were vital to the growth of maize and other crops. Associated with this cardinal point was the color white, which even in European cultures has always symbolized cold, snow, and ice.

Like the Aztec, the Maya attributed to white the meaning of royalty and purity. In fact, refined white cotton dresses were worn only by members of the elite. Common people could not afford this privilege, and dressed in clothing made of rough fabrics from agave fibers.

The expression "white flower" referred to the soul and the spirit, which stressed even more this color's intrinsic meaning of sacredness and spirituality. In decoration, we find the color white in shell, bone mosaics, and in the white feathers of aquatic birds such as the heron.

Inscriptions often mentioned specific place names—the "white house," the "white mountain," "white water"; these had particularly positive connotations, in contrast with other places that were identified as black, thus negative, threatening connotations. The water of lakes and ponds where purifying ablutions took place and where water lilies floated was referred to as white; by contrast, the dark waters of the sacrificial wells where people were thrown to their death and the kingdom of the dead were black.

White was also used to describe the White Road, which in Yucatec is written sak be. This was the name the Maya gave to the Milky Way, which they observed together with many other stars and planets, knowledge of which they transmitted to the Aztec. To the Milky Way they associated the god Mixcoatl, literally, "Cloud Snake." The Milky Way was conceived in different fashions, but in any case, undoubtedly, the Maya believed it was a real road, which led to Xibalbá.

Thus King Pacal is depicted on the Palenque stone slab sliding along the Milky Way, the long white road in the celestial vault which leads to the afterlife and the abode of the gods. This theory, to which perhaps not every scholar subscribes, offers suggestive elements for the study of Maya astronomy.

The Maya greatly valued shells, which they finely engraved, such as the lovely example on the left. Some types of shells were made into white jewels, with fragments used on feathers, jade, and turquoise, creating stunning mosaics.

CENTER—BLUE AND GREEN

The glyph for "center," that is, the living world, was associated with the glyph for the colors blue and green. The Maya treated them as a single color, and they even had the same word for them: yax.

The Maya universe was divided into three separate, distinct worlds: the Upper World was the celestial sphere, the realm of the gods; the Center World was the earth, where mortals lived. Finally, there was the Lower World, the realm of the dead, also called Xibalbá. Sometimes the world of the living was represented as the back of a caiman or a turtle carapace. Oriented to the four directions, its cardinal points were supported by four mythical Bacab, who had been placed there at the time of creation and whose task was to support the sky vault.

Each cardinal point was associated with a color, a tree, and a bird. In the center of the four directions was the Cosmic Tree. This was the universal axis, understood as a gigantic ceiba tree enriched with cosmogonic and mythological attributes, or as the Great Cross, such as the one carved on the temple of the same name and on the Palenque sarcophagus.

In Maya philosophy, the tree dug its roots in the netherworld and stretched its branches up to the Upper World, while the trunk crossed the earth. To cross from one universe to the other, souls and gods slid along the red lymph of the tree, symbol of blood and of life. The concept of center, represented by the sacred tree or the cruciform axis, was in all probability the central concept of Maya cosmogony, around which everything else revolved and from which the four directions of the cardinal points branched out.

The two colors associated with the center, blue and green, were treated by the Maya as one color, using the same glyph to express them. In Yucatec the colors were known as yax. This word also appears in the names of some rulers, for example, one of Copán's kings was Yax Kuk Mo', which means "Blue Macaw Quetzal."

Blue predominated in the frescoes and vase paintings of the Maya. It was extracted from a special clay mixed with a type of musk and took

Detail from a page of the Madrid Codex, *showing a water goddess highlighted in blue. The colors blue and green were charged with symbolism and were represented by turquoise and jade, respectively.*

Turquoise became popular especially beginning with the Postclassic period. The tail feathers of the quetzal bird, a symbol of power worn exclusively by kings, were a brilliant emerald green.

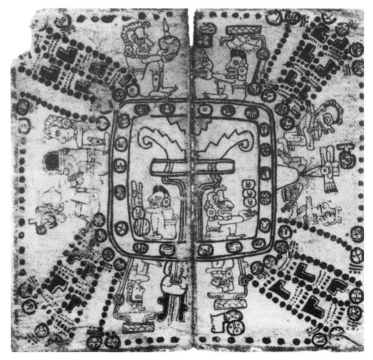

on such an unusual, luminous shade that it was called "Maya blue." We can admire this color in the frescoes decorating the walls of tombs and temples, and especially in pottery objects, among them, the elegant Jaina-style artifacts. Blue painted figures also appear in the codices. From descriptions in Classic period texts, we know that the blue feathers of the quetzal and the Ara macaw were highly sought after as trimming for headdresses and ceremonial attire.

According to Diego de Landa, in the Postclassic era and possibly earlier, blue was the sacrificial color of choice. The victims, the altars, even the priests of Chichén Itzá and Uxmal were covered with blue ointment to prepare them for cruel human sacrifices. The incense tablets found at the bottom of the sacred cenote were also blue. Finally, during the celebrations dedicated to the god Chac, which took place in the months of Yax and Mol, there was a ritual, called the distribution of the color blue, which consisted of sprinkling this color on men and objects, probably for cleansing

purposes. Chac was the god of rain, and turquoise was a clear reference to the clean, limpid water that falls from the sky.

Like the ancient Chinese, the Maya believed that green, like turquoise, was closely linked to water, the life-giving, purifying element that made maize and all other plants grow. The symbolic importance of this color was represented by jade, the semi-precious stone that the Maya considered even more precious than gold. Countless jewels, masks, and divine effigies made of jade were recovered in tombs, evidence of the spiritual significance this semi-precious stone had acquired. Finally, the tail feathers of the quetzal bird were also a bright emerald green; they were worn exclusively by royal officials to symbolize, a meaning the Maya people have retained to this day.

Above: *Mask made of a green stone similar to jade.*
Right: *Pages 75 and 76 of the* Madrid Codex *illustrating gods, cardinal-point ceremonies and the Center, represented by a quadrilateral with the Cosmic Tree in its center and flanked on each side by the supreme god Itzamná and his wife, Ix Chel. Madrid, Museo de América.*

ONE

TWO

In Maya the number one was signified by the word hun and was written as a dot. The concept of "one" and of "unique" is found in the myth of creation in Maya cosmogony: the *Chilam Balam* narrates that "Where there was neither earth nor sky, the first word of God resounded. He was the Uncreated God, the Unique God, Hunab Ku, the Great Hand, the Heart of the Earth." Like the corresponding Aztec god Omeotl, Hunab Ku, while being one, was also dual, as he also embodied his feminine version. The myth of the one god or of the divine couple is very ancient and common to all Mesoamerican cultures.

This god, or his feminine version, was the patron of the first day of Tzolkin, the ritual calendar, and was associated with the caiman, which was the symbol of the earth. Thus, the concept of one was bound with that of origin, although it was perceived as a divisible number. In particular, it was the meeting of two or four opposites, the center of the world's axis, the heart of the Cosmic Tree.

The glyph for number one consisted of a dot. In Maya it was expressed by the word *hun*.

The number two was expressed by two dots. This number was central to the Maya mathematical system, which was vigesimal, twenty being the second-order unit—unlike today's Western system, which is decimal, with the second-order unit being the number ten.

The principle of duality and the double is present throughout Maya religion and cosmogony. Rather than being unique, each deity was believed to be divisible into its double or dual version, whether female or male. One recurring example in all the cultures of pre-Columbian America is the dualism of sun and moon, who were thought of as groom and bride, brother and sister. In recounting the creation myth, the *Popol Vuh* mentions the twins Hunahpu and Xbalanque, "true gods" who destroyed the family of giants who had ruled the earth before them. Another mythical couple was that of the peccaries, which some scholars have identified in the symbol for the constellation of Orion. "Eb Two made the first staircase, and lowered his deity in the middle of the sky" (from *Chilam Balam*).

The glyph for the number two consisted of two dots: Two was double, dualism, the foundation of the system based on the number twenty.

Left: *A vase painting of Hunab Ku, the First Creator Being, in the guise of the young maize god "resurrecting" to new life by splitting his own skull.*

Right: *Postclassic vase painting of two hunters in ceremonial dress.*

THREE

FOUR

The number three was indicated by three dots. It referred to the vertical division of the universe, made up of the

Three was the key number in Maya cosmogony: its glyph consisted of three dots.

netherworld, the earth inhabited by human beings, and the Upper World, which was the abode of the gods. Three was the square root of nine, thus it was considered the set of two opposites plus the center. Inscriptions frequently mentioned places or people whose names contained the number three.

Concerning religion, we recall here the special cult of the Palenque Triad, consisting of three similar deities whose precise identity is still unknown, who were worshiped by the Palenque rulers as their three ancestors, deified founders of the royal lineage. Chan Bahlum, the son of King Pacal, had three temples built and dedicated to these deities. "Ben Three made all of these things, all things, those of the heavens, the seas, and the earth" *(Chilam Balam).*

Vase painting with Xib Chac, one of the gods of the Palenque Triad, in the center. The members of the triad have not been identified.

Four was also an important number for the Maya, the sacred number to which all of creation belonged. It was expressed by four dots.

The number four, represented by four dots, symbolized the division of the universe into four parts.

One and the Center were not understood as concepts in and of themselves, but only as quadripartite entities. The universe was composed of four parts—the center with the four cardinal points—each corner supported by a Bacab, who was one manifestation of the Chac god. Thus, the number four was the four directions, the four extremities of the cross and of the world's axis. Its patron was

Vase painted with a floral motif: four flowers are visible on the outside surface, each with four petals.

Kinich Ahau, the god of the divine sun.

According to Maya mythology (and Aztec as well), there were four creations, four different eras at the dawn of history. *Popol Vuh* recounts the history of the very first men whom the gods created. The "four maize men" were fashioned by the gods with white and yellow maize that four animals had found: the jaguar, the coyote, the parrot, and the crow. "It happened that on the fourth of Ix heaven and earth met, and bowed to each other" *(Chilam Balam).*

FIVE

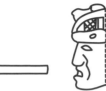

SIX

The number five was represented by a bar, which could be vertical or horizontal. It was conceived as the symbol of the cross, formed by the **The graphic symbol for number five was a bar. Mesoamerican people believed they were living in the fifth creation.** four directions plus the center. Both the Maya and the Aztec believed they were living in the fifth era or fifth creation, that of the "movement sun," born of the movement and union of the elements that had unsuccessfully attempted to form the preceding eras.

The last month of the solar year, called Uayeb, consisted of five days that were believed to be inauspicious. The astronomers subdivided the 260-day ritual calendar, called Tzolkin, into various phases or periods. The division into five parts became important because it resulted into fifty-two–day cycles, which were related to the fifty-two–year cycles (the calendar rounds) of the Long Count.

The number five appears with reference to many places, both real and supernatural, mentioned in inscriptions. In Copán and Palenque there are frequent references to "the house of five flowers" and "the place of five flowers," in all likelihood imaginary places. Elsewhere, a "mountain of the five flowers" was also mentioned.

The number six was indicated by a dot (the value of one) plus a bar (the value of five). It is found as part of geographical names mentioned in inscriptions, whose meaning is still unknown, such "the place of the six **The number six glyph consisted of the bar for number five together with the dot for number one. Its value consisted in the fact that it was the product of two and three.** shells in the hand" or "the place of the six black water surfaces." This last expression possibly refers to six sacred wells and to a city or place where cenote worship was very important, but we have neither the real name of the city nor its location. In any case, number six had no particular meaning, being considered above all a multiple of two and three. Says the *Chilam Balam:* "Cib Six was for the first time light, where there was neither sun nor moon."

A page from the Dresden Codex *with a number of calculations about the cycle of Venus, who is personified in these illustrations along with the moon goddess. The graphic signs of numbers five and six are repeated several times.*

SEVEN

EIGHT

The number seven was expressed by a bar and two dots. From an analysis of historical and mythological texts, where it appears frequently, we

The number seven, whose graphic representation was a bar and two dots, had a deep esoteric meaning.

can reasonably infer that for the Maya this number was imbued with religious and esoteric significance. Interestingly, this is also true of the Judeo-Christian Bible and many sacred books of the ancient East. Seven is also the number of stars making up the Pleiades constellation, which the Maya astronomers knew and studied.

The third part of *Popol Vuh* narrates the epic of the original tribes who founded the Quiché Maya people, when they were looking for a place where they could settle. Their final destination was Vucub Pec, the "seven caves," Vucub Zuivan, the "seven ravines," and other places whose names contained the sacred number. The Aztec Nahuatl myths refer to a similar place, called Chicomotzoc, which means "the place of the seven caves." Finally, the *Annals of the Cakchiquels* recount the history of the seven tribes who came in from the sea in search of a new fatherland. In this case also, they were the founding tribes of the Quiché Maya.

The number eight was indicated by a bar and three dots. It was not considered important in itself, being specifically the

Eight, represented by a bar plus three dots, was considered primarily a multiple of two and four.

product of two and four. In astronomy, it was connected to the Venusian cycle because the 2,920-day period in which the planet's synodic revolution took place corresponded exactly to eight solar calendar years (8 x 365 = 2,920).

"Etz-nab Eight rested his head and his foot, which it set on the earth," thus is written in

Drawing from a stele; it is the glyph of a name-place that means "house subdivision."

the *Chilam Balam.* And with reference to the Katun 8 Ahau, the book says: "Katun 8 Ahau is the ninth Katun. Itzmal is the seat of Katun. Kinich Kakmó Fire-Altar-with-the-Sunny-Face! Arrows will fall after the king of the land! They will set their head in the regions of the

plains and she will be the lady of the land. It will be the end of oppression and of bad luck for everyone!"

Vase painted scene of two men on either side of a stone staircase, about to begin a ball game. They *were possibly two Popol Vuh characters, One Hunahpu and Seven Hunahpu.*

NINE

The number nine was expressed by a bar and four dots. Like two, four, seven, and twenty, it was a major number in the Mayan calendar system and in their vision of the cosmos.

According to the Maya, the Lower World was divided into nine layers, each one supported by its own guardian god. These gods were known as Bolontikú, which means "the nine gods"; these stood opposite the thirteen patron gods of heaven's upper layers. Each of the nine gods was also the patron of each of the hours into which the night was subdivided.

Although scholars have succeeded in identifying the name glyphs for the Bolontikú in the codices, their names and images are still unknown. The texts mention only the last one, Mitnal, who lived in the deepest layer, often identified with the god of death. In two temples—at Yaxchilán and Palenque respectively—traces of nine individuals, probably the nine Bolontikú, have been detected, but as yet there is no identification of their features. In the Postclassic period nine was considered a magic number in medicine and witchcraft.

Nine, represented by a bar and four dots, was a central number in Maya cosmogony.

The jaguar god appears as decoration on this vase. He guarded the netherworld and was associated with Mitnal, the lord of the ninth layer of the Lower World.

TEN

The number ten was represented by two bars, twice five, and its guardian was the god of death. From a mathematical point of view, the value of ten was lower than twenty, its multiple, since the Mayan numerical system was based on the number twenty. The 260-day ritual calendar, which was usually divided by four, by five, by thirteen, and by twenty, was also divided by ten in the *Dresden Codex* (10 x 26).

The number ten, represented by two bars, was considered a multiple of five. The patron god of number ten was the god of death.

An image of the death god, guardian of number ten, dancing a macabre dance, in a scene probably taken from Popol

Vuh. *Next to the skeleton is a dog who, as the Greco-Roman Cerberus, was the guardian of the entrance to the netherworld.*

ELEVEN

TWELVE

The number eleven was expressed by two bars and a dot. The number is quoted in the *Chilam Balam* in the chapter relating the prophecies for Katun 11 Ahau, described as a new, "luminous" cycle that succeeded the preceding inauspicious *katun*. The scriptures read: "When the time came for the following *katun,* since the *katun* during which the dishonest had been led was ended, we saw their many warriors. Katun 11 Ahau sits on the mat, he sits on the throne. There he raises his voice, there he raises his lordship. His god's face sends forth rays. Leaves fall from the sky, flowery arches fall from the sky. He wears a heavenly perfume."

The number eleven was represented graphically by two bars, each representing five, plus a dot.

The number twelve was expressed by two bars and two dots. In the Haab, the Maya solar calendar, the year consisting of 360 days plus five was not subdivided into twelve months of thirty or thirty-one days each (as in the Gregorian calendar) but in eighteen twenty-day months, plus a very short last month of five days, which were considered to be inauspicious. Thus the value of number twelve was important for the Maya only because it was a multiple of three, which expressed the two opposites plus the center, and of four, which expressed the four directions.

"On the twelfth Ik the wind was born, thus its name was born: wind, spirit, because inside of him he was not dead." This is what is written in the *Chilam Balam* about number twelve. This number recurs frequently in the codices in the context of oracles and rituals, and was associated with special deities and animals. As a multiple of four, it recalled the entire universe, consisting of the world of the living, the Upper World, and the netherworld.

The number twelve, a product of the key numbers three and four, was less important than thirteen. It was denoted by two bars and two dots.

Number twelve was a multiple of two, three and four, each a key numeral in Maya cosmogony. Numbers eleven and twelve appear with the other numbers in this astronomical scene from the Madrid Codex. The maize god can be seen on the right in the act of sowing kernels, preparing the furrows with a large stick. In all likelihood, this painted scene and its calendrical calculations were related to agricultural cycles.

THIRTEEN

FOURTEEN

Undoubtedly the number thirteen was a sacred number for the Maya and the Aztec, imbued with deep esoteric meaning,

Thirteen was considered a magical number. It was denoted by two bars and three dots.

as it was for all ancient and modern cultures of the Old World. Chac, the god of rain and fertility, was the patron god of thirteen.

This number was indirectly linked to the fundamental principle of the four directions, inasmuch as it was considered the set of three four-number combinations (twelve), plus the center, where the highest god resided. As with nine, the number thirteen also partook of the cosmogonic subdivision of the universe: the Maya worshiped the thirteen gods of the Upper World who ruled over the thirteen layers or "skies" into which the Upper World was subdivided. These gods were called Olontikú, and they were believed to be opposite to the nine Bolontikú, set at the antipodes of the netherworld.

We have no knowledge of the name glyphs of the thirteen Olontikú, nor of how they were represented. According to some scholars, they were ancestral deities who might have been high on the divine hierarchy at the dawn of Maya civilization. There is some evidence for this theory in the *Chilam Balam*. They were also the patron gods of the thirteen hours into which the day was subdivided.

The number thirteen supported the computations of the calendar. In all of Mesoamerica, since the time of the Olmec the 260-day ritual calendar was separated into thirteen periods of twenty days each, which were called months. In addition, dividing 260 by twenty produced twenty thirteen-day groups.

The Maya expressed the number fourteen with two bars and four dots, i.e., ten plus four units. This number was important because it was a multiple of seven, however it was not a major number since it was not linked to any particular esoteric meaning.

The number fourteen was not particularly important, except that it was a multiple of seven.

Thirteen in the Aztec world

This illustration shows the "first thirteen," namely, the first thirteen-year computation of the Aztec calendar. Four glyphs are used, each marked by a number made up of from one to thirteen dots. When each year received its thirteen-number series, a fifty-two-year cycle was completed (13 x 4).

FIFTEEN

SIXTEEN

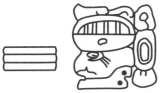

The number fifteen was expressed by three bars, equivalent to three times five. Once again, the importance of this number lay primarily in the fact that it was the product of three and five, two key numbers in Maya religion and astronomy. The number fifteen is rarely cited in sacred texts, probably because it was not endowed with any specific esoteric meaning. One rare example in which it appears in a sacred text is in a page from the *Chilam Balam,* where it is linked to other key numbers: "And then the great Itzaes left. They had lived as heretics for thirteen times four hundred times, four hundred thousand and fifteen times four hundred times four hundred hundreds." Thus in this text, the number fifteen is mentioned together with thirteen, a sacred number, and four hundred, an important multiple of twenty in Maya calendrical computations and mythological texts.

The number fifteen was represented graphically by three bars, i.e., three times five.

The number sixteen, expressed by three bars and a dot, sometimes appears as a key number in Maya culture. First, it is a multiple of four, which symbolizes the quadripartite division of the universe. That may be the reason why this number appears in the dimensions of sacred buildings, such as the pyramid on which the Temple of Inscriptions in Palenque rises. Moreover, the city of Tikal covered an area of about six square miles (16 sq. km). The large rectangular stone altar built in Copán during the Classic age is decorated by an elegant relief depicting all the monarchs who took the throne, each sitting and richly dressed, with his name glyph at his side. The Copán dynasty included exactly sixteen kings. Yax Pac was the sixteenth and last king before the decline set in.

The number sixteen, represented graphically by three bars and a dot, was an important number, being a multiple of four.

The reliefs of Copán's Altar Q portray all the kings of the city's reigning dynasty. On the far right is the fifteenth king,

Smoking Shell and to his left is the sixteenth king, accepting the scepter from Yax Kuk Mo', the dynasty's founder.

SEVENTEEN

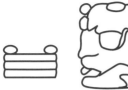

The Maya expressed the number seventeen as three bars and two dots. This number was not particularly relevant for astronomy or the calendar, nor did it have any esoteric

This number was represented by three bars and two dots. The seventeenth day of Tzolkin was dedicated to the moon goddess.

meaning. Unlike essential numbers such as thirteen, nine, and fourteen, it appears infrequently in the *Popol Vuh* and the *Chilam Balam.* The seventeenth day of Tzolkin, the Maya ritual calendar, called Caban, was dedicated to the moon goddess, in its manifestation as the crescent moon.

The rabbit was a frequent subject of vase paintings, as this drawing illustrates. In addition to being the scribe god, he was associ- *ated with the cult of the crescent moon, to which the seventeenth day of the ritual calendar was dedicated.*

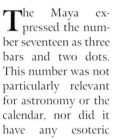

EIGHTEEN

This number was especially important, insofar as it was a multiple of the key numbers three and nine: it was represented by three bars and three dots.

The number eighteen, a multiple of three and nine, was expressed by three bars and three dots. It was an important number in the solar calendar.

The number eighteen was also important in computing the solar calendar: this calendar consisted of eighteen twenty-day periods—which we would consider "months"—and one additional very short period of five days, bringing the total number of days to 365.

A drawing of a calendrical glyph which refers to the date 18 Cumku, part of the Initial Series found on Stele F in Quiriguá.

Additionally, the symbol for the number eighteen appears as part of the name glyph of a very important ruler of the city of Copán: archaeologists have given the name Eighteen Rabbit to this ruler. Archaeological and epigraphic evidence speaks of him as a true enlightened king. It was during his forty-three–year reign that the city of Copán reached its architectural and political apogee. We do not know the true name of this famous individual.

NINETEEN

TWENTY

This the last number expressed by the use of dots and bars. Although not a particularly relevant number for the Maya,

Nineteen is the last number of the Maya arithmetical system represented by dots and bars.

we should note that the solar calendar, in addition to the eighteen months of twenty days each, also included a very brief month, the nineteenth, consisting of five unlucky days. This nineteenth month was called Uayeb, which in Yucatec Maya means "the sleeping one." The number nineteen was followed by a key number for the Maya: the number twenty, represented graphically with a special symbol. Maya astronomers were able to perform highly complex calculations that helped them understand the cycles of the planets, the sun, and the moon.

As mentioned in the introduction to this chapter, the number twenty was a fundamental number for the Maya, who never used the decimal

Twenty was a key number in the Maya vigesimal system. The codices often represented it with the moon glyph.

metric system, but like other Mesoamerican populations, always based their astronomical and calendar calculations on base twenty since the dawn of their civilization. The number twenty could be expressed in a calculation by writing the unit dot in the second place. More often, though, it was expressed by the moon symbol.

While from the beginning of time Europeans have divided time into decades, centuries, and millennia, the Maya registered its course in twenty-year cycles—the *katun*—and in four-hundred-year periods —the *baktun*. We will discuss this further in a later chapter. The number twenty was the point of departure for the two most important Maya calendrical computations, in particular the ritual calendar—called Tzolkin—which was based on a twenty-day cycle. The number four hundred, considered to be the most important multiple of twenty, recurs often in sacred texts and inscriptions.

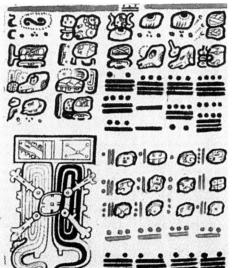

A page from the Dresden Codex *with the symbol of a solar eclipse and a series of astronomical calculations in which the numbers nineteen and twenty appear often, the latter expressed by the moon's stylized glyph.*

ZERO

Zero, or the completion, was "invented" by the Maya many centuries before its discovery by the mathematicians of the Old World. To the left are two symbols that represented zero: half of a four-petal flower, and a three-petal flower.

In Western culture, zero, or nought, expresses the absence of any value, quantity, or unit. The symbol "o" was conceived by Indian mathematicians in the fifth century A.D. and introduced in Europe by the Arabs only in the eighth century A.D. Although it may seem surprising, the zero symbol was adopted many centuries earlier in Mesoamerica. Like the entire base-twenty mathematical system, calendrical computations and script, in all probability the number zero dates to the Preclassic period, and is derived in all likelihood from the Olmec and Zapotec cultures.

Several glyphs were used in inscriptions and codices to express zero: the most common symbol was that of the shell, Ximim in Yucatec, or the stylized symbol of half of a four-petal flower.

The value and meaning the Maya attributed to zero was totally unlike the significance it had in the Arabic numbering system adopted in the Europe. Rather than

A relief from a tablet from the Palace in Palenque showing a "full-figure glyph," meaning figures with both human and animal features. The calendar notation "zero days" is represented by the zero god wearing a stylized flower on his arms, together with the monkey god expressing the word "day."

Together with other symbols, the shell (ximim in Yucatec) was also a symbol for the number zero. Above are drawings after some very stylized shell glyphs; below is a "flowery" shell, a typical motif in Classic relief decorations.

indicating nothing or the absence of quantity or units, it expressed the completion of a series. Thus, the Maya had conceived the number zero to complete a numerical series in the calendrical Long Count: it was used to close a type of quantitative unit by carrying it forward to a higher unit. The number zero was also used to multiply units, with a method like that of the current decimal system.

RELIGION

The Maya gods were infinite, for they believed supernatural beings were endowed with the power of taking on multiple aspects in each and all natural elements, in water, in the mountains, and in the stars. Shamans went into a state of trance in order to make contact with deities through the *nahual,* symbolic totemic animals of Mesoamerican religion.

GODS AND CULTS

The subject of Maya religion can best be approached by briefly referring to the beliefs of other pre-Columbian American populations. For there is a common substratum to Peruvian, Amazonian, Mesoamerican and, possibly, North American Indian cultures. For many years, scholars have been searching for the origin of this substratum and how it was possible for iconographies and religious cults to spread throughout such a vast territory. Ethnography, archaeological sources, and the history at the time of the conquest have allowed us to reconstruct this fascinating mosaic only in part. The very recent, though partial, deciphering of ancient scripts of the Maya, Inca, and Aztec, is providing a precious tool for understanding complex ideologies that are often vastly different from contemporary Western culture.

When we speak of religion in the pre-Columbian world, we mean not just a group of humanized or anthropomorphic deities, but rather a concept of sacredness with which each thing and each aspect of life was endowed. Animals, plants, the stars, rocks, natural phenomena, everything was sacred. The "divine breath," understood in the broad sense, was present everywhere, and each divine being, the gods themselves, the kings, and the shamans all had an animal double.

Historical and literary sources have enabled scholars to learn about some aspects of Maya religion. We have, first of all, the reports of the first European clerics, for exmple Diego de Landa, who described Maya Postclassic rituals and beliefs, by then already permeated with Toltec elements. The sacred Maya scriptures

The last page of the Dresden Codex. Elegantly painted, it depicts a reptilian being rising from gushing water, possibly a symbol of the Deluge. The Deluge myth appears in Maya religion and cosmogony, as it does throughout the Old World.

Popol Vuh and *Chilam Balam*, which are copies made by native scribes of Maya religious texts transcribed into the Latin alphabet, and the four original surviving codices, contain literary narratives as well as true divination almanacs. These sources, which point to the inseparable link between gods, the calendar, and astronomy, are often corroborated by archaeological evidence such as the images of gods and religious rituals found on reliefs, burial chamber walls, and pottery.

A terra-cotta vessel from the early Classic period with a monster, possibly the Quadripartite Monster, with a jaguar coming from his jaws. An important cult was dedicated to this deity.

From a review of images and an interpretation of glyphs, archaeologists have been able to corroborate that each and every festival, act of worship, or religious sacrifice was intimately linked to temporal cycles and the position of the heavenly bodies. Each heavenly phenomenon had a special meaning, and each star and planet its own deity.

A cylindrical vase with polychrome drawings on a white background. The bird is possibly the mythical muan, a divine being of the Maya cosmogony. Guatemala City, Museo Popol Vuh.

According to the most reliable theories, Maya religion is rooted in Olmec religion and is based on the cult of the Jaguar, on shamanism as well as *nahualism*. The latter is the belief that each deity had an animal double that allowed it to come into contact with men through hallucinatory rituals. In addition to shamans, beginning with the Classic period there came into existence a true priestly caste, whose members were in charge of worship and guarding the temples, in addition to a caste of scribes and teachers of divination.

Many Maya deities correspond to deities worshiped by the Aztec and other Mesoamerican peoples. Of these, the most important was Chac-Tlaloc, the rain god, in whose honor cruel sacrifices were offered even up to the end of the Postclassic age. There is a lovely painting on the walls of Teotihuacan of the so-called Tlaloc Paradise.

One unique aspect of this religion was that each deity had two, even four aspects. And in addition to what we would consider true gods, Maya cosmogony also included supernatural beings. Represented by a complex iconography, these stood for the divine aspect of natural elements such as water, mountains,

Postclassic stone sculpture of a man inside a snake's jaws. In this period the ancient Maya gods were replaced by the cult of Quetzalcoatl-Kukulkan, the Toltec feathered snake god. Uxmal, Pyramid of the Magician.

the serpent, the sky, and the earth. These elements, thus transformed into monstrous beings, became symbols and intermediaries for moving between the earth and the supernatural world. At the point of death, the soul left the body and entered Xibalbá, the realm of the afterlife, where it remained until the time came for it to reincarnate itself on earth.

The sacred book of *Popol Vuh,* a sort of Bible of the Guatemalan Quiché Maya, narrates the events of man's creation. It was said that the gods fashioned man out of maize, so that he might use it as an object of worship and honor them. The god who created man was Hunab Ku, considered an abstract entity, much higher than all the other gods and so detached from everything that its representation was impossible.

In the course of centuries, the pantheon of Maya religion grew increasingly larger. To the ancestral gods, rooted in an Olmec substratum, other deities were added until the Toltec domination, at which time Kukulkan, the Feathered Serpent, became the dominant god.

Certain theories hold that Kukulkan had already been worshiped in very ancient times, as we can deduce from ancient Preclassic iconographies. It certainly had become an important cult in Teotihuacan, and their people transmitted this worship to the Toltec of the city of Tula.

ITZAMNÁ
THE SUPREME GOD

The two glyphs on the left represent the supreme god, Itzamná, the first god, father of all the gods, who appeared under multiple guises: monotheism and dualism, scriptures and divination.

Of all the gods, Itzamná was in all probability worshiped as the first god, the creator god of the many manifestations. His figure embodied monotheism and polytheism; both principles belong to Maya culture and are concepts proper to a dualistic conception of the world. Like Kukulkan, Itzamná is depicted with snake-like features. His name means Reptile House or, more correctly, according to some scholars, Iguana House.

In Maya cosmology, the serpent symbolized heaven as well as earth and the netherworld; the creator god included all of these aspects within himself. As an embodiment of heavenly paradise, he was portrayed with one or more serpent-like dragons springing from his mouth. As an embodiment of the afterlife, he took on the image of a skeleton or water reptile, often the caiman.

In the *Popol Vuh* it is said that Itzamná fashioned man out of maize paste. Itzamná was associated with the sun deities, and his bride, Ix Chel, the moon's heavenly mother, was also the patron goddess of female fertility. The cult of this god was strictly linked to that of the ruling Maya dynasties and he was considered their most important protector. In all probability, one of Itzamná's symbols was the two-headed snake appearing on the ceremonial rod that many dignitaries carry in Copán's reliefs.

Many ceremonies celebrating the beginning of the new year were connected to this god. During such ceremonies, he was invoked to ward off danger and calamities, while during the celebrations of the various months he was worshiped under its many other manifestations, such as the sun god or the guardian of medicine. In Maya religion, the role of Itzamná was always positive: unlike those of other gods, his images were never linked with death or war.

In vase paintings of the late Classic period Itzamná is represented as a scribe. Several pages of the four surviving codices describe him as a high ranking, priestly individual. Such images are confirmed in Postclassic Yucatec religion, when Itzamná was worshiped as the first priest of mankind, the inventor of writing. It is reasonable to presume that in this last phase of Maya civilization, the cult of Itzamná had been merged with that of Quetzalcoatl-Kukulkan, since they were both positive gods who dispensed artistic and scientific knowledge.

The Itzamná god, as illustrated in the codex, next to two name glyphs. This complex deity had snake-like attributes and was the guardian of writing and the divinatory arts.

CHAC
GOD OF RAIN

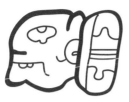

Chac, the god of rain and fertility, was worshiped under different names in all of Mesoamerica since ancient times. Many rituals that invoked abundant harvests were dedicated to him.

After Itzamná, Chac is the god that appears most frequently in the four codices, where its image recurs 218 times. In Maya territories, as well as in the rest of Mesoamerica, rain deities filled a very important role, since it was rain that made the fields fertile, gave life, and brought prosperity. The whole population, the peasants in particular, dedicated many rituals and ceremonies to this god, especially during the months of Chen and Yax. The day Ik and the number thirteen were also dedicated to him.

The sacred animals of this god, which were also his stand-ins, were especially the frog and the turtle, both aquatic animals. In Peru, Colombia, and Ecuador, a cult of the frog and the toad was also practiced, for these animals were believed to ensure an abundant supply of water, so important in farming.

Chac was portrayed with a monstrous face with reptilian features and a prominent nose like an elephant's trunk, sometimes even with curved tusks. Images of this god began to appear frequently on pottery and on buildings, primarily at the end of the Classic period. Large relief masks with his image, recognizable by the long trunk, are found on temples decorated in the late Puuc style. At a later date, Chac probably merged with the Mexican god Tlaloc, who had been imposed by the Toltec invaders who had been worshiping him centuries earlier in Teotihuacan. The worship of this god continued to be important in Chichén Itzá, where many victims were sacrificed to him by throwing them into the murky waters of the cenote, in an attempt to ward off famine and drought.

Chac is also important in Maya cosmogony. Like other supernatural beings, he was both a single and a quadripartite god: to each of his four divine manifestations was associated a color and a cardinal point.

Detail from a Madrid Codex page: the Chac god with the prominent trunk-like snout is painted blue—the symbolic color of water and purification—and shown pouring water. He is supported by the blue snake of water and purification.

YUM CIMIL
GOD OF DEATH

The god of death was represented by two name glyphs: one is the head of a corpse with closed eyes, the other is the head of the god and recurs frequently in the codices.

Yum Cimil (or God A), the name given to the god of death, comes from the Yucatec. Mention of this god recurs frequently in the codices, eighty-eight times to be exact. Together with Itzamná, he is the only god with two name glyphs: the first is the stylized head of a corpse with closed eyes; the second reproduces the head of the god with a truncated nose, sunken jaws, and a symbol of the sacrificial knife. It is a gruesome skeletal image. Sometimes the god is shown dancing with other macabre denizens of the netherworld.

Often, the image of God A is associated with that of God F, the god of war and human sacrifices. For the Maya, the concept of death was inevitably linked with the ritual of sacrifice, where the victims were often captured war enemies. Several small copper and gold rattles have been recovered from Chichén Itzá's sacred sacrificial well, the cenote, into which men and women were thrown to their death in the name of this god. The rattles are probably reproductions of similar objects that appear in Yum Cimil's hair, on his arms, and around his ankles in his various images.

God A was the patron god of the Day of Cimi, which means death, and the number ten. In one of his manifestations he ruled the lowest of the nine Lower Worlds, the Mitnal. His *nahual,* the animals that were his double, were the muan and the owl, two birds believed to be inauspicious. The corresponding god in Aztec religion was probably Mictlantécuhtli, which means "lord of Mictlan," the kingdom of the dead in Mexican cultures, similar to the Maya's Xibalbá. Other Mesoamerican civilizations, such as that of Veracruz, worshiped a god with a skeletal image, who nevertheless did not seem threatening.

We already discussed at some length the subject of death, a vast, complex issue in Mesoamerican cultures. We should simply note here that the Maya attributed great importance to death and burial, to guarantee to the deceased a safe passage to Xibalbá. Many scenes from vase paintings depict the god of death as a skeleton dancing his macabre dance together with other deities and with a dog that was entrusted with watching over the souls of the deceased.

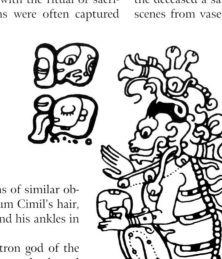

The god of death, portrayed in the codices as a squatting skeletal being, appears often in scenes of human sacrifice.

EK CHUAH
GOD OF MERCHANTS

The Maya considered the god of merchants to also be the patron of the cocoa plant. Sometimes his glyph is associated with that of the North Star, the guiding star of seafarers and travelers.

Like the gods of beekeeping, war, and weaving, this deity was among the group of divine patrons of the arts and crafts. Following in the footsteps of the Olmec, since the dawn of their civilization the Maya had been active traders, using all available waterways. Their most important currencies were cocoa, jade, feathers, shells, and obsidian. Since there were no pack animals in pre-Columbian America, all goods were carried on men's backs. When the goods were shipped on waterways, the Maya used log canoes, which they probably equipped with sails in later periods.

The patron god of merchants appears often in the codices. He is usually painted black and shown with a drooping lower lip and a load, a sack of merchandise, on his back. His name symbol is a black-circled eye. In some cases, his image is coupled with the god of the North Star, who served as night guide to traveling merchants. Ek Chuah was also worshiped by the cocoa growers, given that the fruit of this plant was a major trade item. The Maya dedicated a feast to Ek Chuah during the month of Muan,

with propitiatory sacrifices and rituals to promote the growing of the precious cocoa beans.

Left: *The god of commerce and cocoa, as portrayed in the* Madrid Codex, *dressed in black. In Maya Yucatec, ek means "black." Madrid, Museo de América.*

Above: *Vase painting of a traveling merchant carrying a load on his shoulders, symbol of the god Ek Chuah.*

IX CHEL
RAINBOW GODDESS

Ix Chel means "Lady Rainbow." This goddess took on multiple aspects, and was intensely worshiped in the Postclassic period as the patron of female fertility and medicine.

Ix Chel, or Lady Rainbow, was a major female goddess. In the Maya religious pantheon, she took on multiple roles, alternatively benign or threatening, depending on the context. For this reason, she is still today an enigmatic figure, since not even her relationship to the rainbow has been explained. She is described in the sacred texts as the bride or female version of Itzamná the creator god.

The image of this deity appears often with that of the war god in scenes of catastrophes and snakes. However, she is also represented as the moon goddess, the female equivalent of the sun, and the guardian of women and childbirth as well as weaving, medicine, and shamanistic healing rituals. At the time of childbirth, midwives dedicated a special ceremony to Ix Chel to ensure the health of both mother and baby.

Only in the Postclassic period is there any firm evidence of her cult. In all likelihood, among the Toltec Maya it replaced a more ancient moon deity, and they built a shrine in her honor on the island of Cozumel, where San Gervasio is located today. At the time of the conquest this religious center had become extremely important as the seat of an oracle for women. Each month, thousands of women landed on the island to consult the goddess and to dance in honor of health and fertility.

The Aztec worshiped a deity who may be considered the equivalent of Ix Chel: it was Cihuacoatl, whose name recalled the concept of snake. Pottery figurines of this goddess were given to women as a good maternity omen.

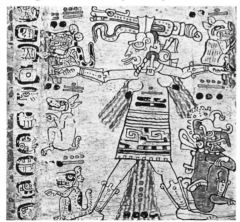

Left: *An illustration from the* Madrid Codex *of the goddess Ix Chel performing a fertility rite associated with a number of mythical animals. Madrid, Museo de América.*

Above: *Ix Chel is still a controversial, manifold figure. Some scholars associate its image with that of the waning moon, contrasting it with the young girl that symbolized the crescent moon.*

MOON GODDESS

The glyph of this ancient deity, whose name is unknown, portrays the stylized face of a young woman, associated with the moon symbol. The corresponding glyph is *na*, "noble lady."

The Maya religious pantheon included some female deities, some of whom have been identified: Ix Tab, the suicide goddess; Ix Chebel Yax, the goddess of weaving; and Ix Chel, the rainbow goddess and bride of Itzamná. This last goddess took on multiple roles, one being to assist women in childbirth. She was also the patron of medicine and witchcraft.

One recurring iconography from the Classic period, whose original name is unknown, has been identified as the moon goddess. She is often mentioned in inscriptions, and is portrayed as a young woman riding a crescent moon and holding a rabbit. Like the ancient Asiatic populations, the Maya believed it was possible to detect the shape of a rabbit in the pockmarked face of the full moon.

The deity's glyph corresponds to the number one and the word *na*, which means "noble lady." For this reason, it was often associated with the names of famous queens, just like the names of important male personalities had the glyph of the sun next to them. In the codices and written sources from the colonial period, the poetic image of a moon-riding girl disappeared, replaced by that of an old, toothless woman, such as the one found on the reliefs of the Temple of the Warriors and Temple of the Jaguars at Chichén Itzá.

The Rabbit and the Moon

The rabbit is a recurring image even in Postclassic iconography. Valued as hunting game, it was associated with god Mixcoatl, guardian of hunters. A Toltec cult that spread to all of central Mexico associated pulque, the fermented drink made from agave leaves, and the agave goddess Mayahuel, in the Myth of the Four Hundred Rabbits. However, the rabbit was the main symbol of the moon until the conquest, according to a very ancient tradition, as illustrated in this detail from the Borgia Codex.

In Classic iconography, the moon goddess was portrayed as a young woman riding the moon with a rabbit in her arms.

In all likelihood, in the Postclassic period this cult was merged with that of Ix Chel, to whom an important sanctuary on Cozumel Island was built, still visited by pilgrims in the sixteenth century.

YUM KAAX
GOD OF MAIZE

The maize god, a handsome young man, was the patron god of the plant he is wearing on his head. Both the plant and the god were expressed by the same glyph. He was also the patron god of farming.

The maize plant, unknown in Europe until the discovery of the New World, was the Maya's main food staple, their nourishment and life. According to *Popol Vuh*, the first men were fashioned out of maize paste; therefore maize was considered holy, a life-generating element like the earth, water, and blood. Thus, the plant had taken on a divine character, and in a later age it was given the name of Yum Kaax. However, the more ancient name, which frequently recurs in codices and on earthenware artifacts, is unknown.

The god was portrayed as a refined-looking youth, wearing an ear of maize on his head and holding another in his hand. He was the patron god of the Kan day, whose glyph *kan* corresponds to that of the maize plant. Yum Kaax was the absolute patron god of agriculture and fieldwork, and appeared often in the codices in the act of sowing.

Classic period reliefs show rulers in the act of nourishing the earth with kernels of maize, as well as with their own blood. Yum Kaax was deemed to be a beneficial god; however he was weak compared to the gods of rain, wind, and death. Before sowing, the Maya would consult astronomical oracles to learn the exact moment when a shower or a storm would help the kernels to sprout more easily.

All pre-Columbian Mesoamerican

cultures have left traces of this worship in their paintings and pottery. The equivalent Aztec god was Cinteotl, also represented as a young man. Most likely, early Mesoamerican societies of the early Preclassic period subsisted on farming, maize crops in particular, which brought about the establishment of rural settlements and, later, of Olmec ceremonial centers.

Above: *A stylized image of Yum Kaax as he appears in the codices, together with his name glyph. The young god carries a maize plant.*

Left: *A lovely ceramic statue of the young, refined-looking god, with a headdress consisting of a maize plant. This plant was sacred since it was the most important agricultural and food staple. Many rituals were intended to drive away the danger of drought and promote abundant harvests.*

KUKULKAN
FEATHERED SERPENT

Kukulkan was the Maya name of the Toltec god Quetzalcoatl, "Quetzal-Feathered Serpent." It was perhaps an extremely ancient cult that demanded bloody sacrifices.

Several scholars have focused their research on Kukulkan, possibly the most complex and puzzling of Mesoamerican gods. This deity was not worshiped by the Maya in the Classic period; his cult was introduced by the Toltec who came from Mexico and forced it on the subjected Maya populations. Worship of this god, together with Tlaloc, came to dominate over time, almost replacing the more ancient deities.

The god's Mexican name was Quetzalcoatl, "Quetzal-Feathered Serpent," since the feathers of the quetzal bird were regarded as the most

Postclassic Maya cities are full of images of the Feathered Serpent, the deity that the Toltec conquerors imposed on them.

precious of all. The Maya changed the name of the foreign god into Kukulkan, keeping the original meaning.

The Toltec and Aztec did not consider Quetzalcoatl merely a god. He was also an ancestral figure, a sort of hero whose origins were lost in the dawn of time and who appeared in different myths. For example, Ce Acatl Quetzalcoatl is the name of an ancient ruler of Tula (an ancient Toltec capital); he was an ascetic, good, and wise man, who taught his subjects arts and sciences. Later expelled by his evil rival Tezcatlipoca ("Smoking Mirror"), Ce Acatl Quetzalcoatl went south to colonize Chichén Itzá. According to another legend, he went to the edge of the sea where he metamorphosed into a feathered serpent with a flaming tail and ascended heaven, where he became the planet Venus.

Out of this tradition, where the historical element meshes with legend, Quetzalcoatl emerges as the serpent god associated with Venus, the Morning Star. We find the serpent image of this deity in Postclassic architecture, especially in Chichén Itzá. Chroniclers reported that even at the time of the conquest, the Maya held cruel, bloody sacrifices and performed self-mutilation to meet the god's unquenchable thirst for blood.

Quetzalcoatl

Who was Quetzalcoatl? Even after extensive research and much debate, it remains an enigmatic figure and cult. According to chroniclers the name Quetzal-Feathered Serpent was given to a cultural hero who was believed to have introduced culture and civilization first to Tula, the Toltec capital, and later to Chichén Itzá. Defeated by his evil brother Tezcatlipoca, he ascended to heaven and metamorphosed into Venus, the Morning Star. The above illustration of the god is taken from Aztec codices.

GOD G 1

This glyph represents the first of the mysterious and complex gods that make up the Palenque Triad, whose original names are unknown, and whose members scholars have called G 1, G 2, and G 3.

The three deities making up what is known as the Palenque Triad (God G 1, God G 2, and God 3) were worshiped as the heavenly ancestors who founded the royal family of that city. We do not know their original names. According to the legend, they were born eighteen days apart, and their parents belonged to a previous creation. Some scholars have identified gods G 1 and G 3 with the two ancestral gods mentioned in *Popol Vuh*.

Although the scholarship is not definite on this point, these three divine beings were probably worshiped as the sacred ancestors not just of Palenque's rulers, but of all the reigning dynasties of the Maya cities during the Classic period.

God G 1 was considered the oldest of the three brothers. Sometimes his name has been translated as Hunahpu, one of the two twin gods of *Popol Vuh*. Like Hunahpu, he was associated with the worship of both the sun and Venus. Rarely found on earthenware objects, his image appears more frequently on Tikal and Copán reliefs, where several rulers are shown wearing his mask. God G 1's face has squarish eyes, the stylized image of a fish stamped on his cheek, a Roman nose, and a shell-shaped ear. His hairstyle is identical to that of another mythical being, the Quadripartite Monster, who in turn is linked to the netherworld and the Milky Way.

Detail of a vase painting depicting a complex macabre dance referring to a Popol Vuh *theme and probably taking place in Xibalbá, the kingdom of the dead. God G 1 is shown in the act of sacrificing the jaguar, symbol of the sun's nightly underground journey. G 1 was associated with the cult of the sun and of Venus.*

GOD G 2

God G 2 is the youngest of the three divine brothers, and the god with the most complex iconography, which includes human and animal elements. The Maya gave him many different names: Tahil, Kauil, Bolon Tzakab, and also Manikin Scepter and Torch God. He was depicted as a human being with a sinuous, snake-like body, one leg ending in a snake's head. His most unusual feature was a mirror-like forehead pierced by an ax, or by a pointed, smoking ax. Sometimes the ax was replaced by a cigar or a torch. The sign representing a torch was, however, a phonetic complement, which aimed to show that the mirror was made of a material whose name

The Maya gave various names to G 2, the second of the Palenque Triad gods.

The complex iconography of God G 2 is that of a sinuous, reptilian being ending with a snake's head.

was analogous in pronunciation to the word *torch* which in Maya is pronounced *tah*. Since *tah* means "obsidian," God G 2 has also been called Obsidian Mirror. For this reason, his image found on ceremonial scepters was connected with self-sacrifice.

GOD G 3

God G 3, the second-born of the three divine brothers, had also a complex imagery. In Palenque's Sun Table he is called Sun Lord or Jaguar Torch Lord. This suggests that he probably took on multiple roles, as also confirmed by inscriptions and by painted images on pottery.

The third deity of the Palenque Triad was known by various names, such as Sun Lord or Jaguar Torch Lord.

The Maya name Ahau Kin, meaning the "Lord Sun" refers to the image of a Roman-profile face, with squarish eyes and a cross-eyed look; the *kin* glyph, which means "day," is imprinted on the cheek or arms, and on his head is a large tuft of hair. God G 3 was considered one manifestation of the sun god and was the patron of number four. He was also depicted as a being with feline traits, who represented an antithetical deity: the Jaguar God of the Night Sun.

God G 3 appears in many forms, such as the baby jaguar, right, with a baby's body and jaguar's tail and paws, or like the water lily jaguar at the left.

GOD OF WAR AND
HUMAN SACRIFICE

The war god was often associated with the death god, also painted black, the color of bad luck and sacrifice. He was also associated with the concept of human sacrifice.

Next to the death god recalled earlier, we frequently find another similar deity in the codices: God F, Buluk Chabtan, patron of war and human sacrifice, who is somehow also connected with death, though in a different way than God A. This deity, the subject of much scholarly debate, is related not so much to death in general, as to, specifically, death on the battlefield or on the sacrificial altar. In her negative manifestation the rainbow goddess, Ix Chel, appears as the bearer of misfortune; she was probably considered the female manifestation of Buluk Chabtan.

In iconography, God F is depicted with a black line surrounding part of the eye and continuing down the cheek. The color black was always present in images of death and adversity. The name glyph consists of the same head together with the number eleven. Additionally, according to tradition, this god was patron of the Manik day, symbolized by a hand in the act of aggressively clutching something. In his most expressive and cruel representation, God F is shown in the act of burning houses with a torch and striking them with a spear, a stylized image that recalls the destruction that follows a battle. The Aztec religious pantheon had sev-

eral deities that corresponded to Buluk Chabtan, examples being the tribal god Huitzilopochtli and the ferocious Tezcatlipoca.

The God of war, as he appears in the Dresden Codex. This god was also associated with the concept of death and human sacrifice. The negative version of goddess Ix Chel was considered this god's female manifestation.

Aztec War Gods

In the complex Aztec religious pantheon two war-related figures emerged, both negative and cruel: Huitzilopochtli and Tezcatlipoca. The former, a sort of devil to the Spanish conquistadors, was the Aztec tribal deity; its name means "southern hummingbird." A temple erected at the top of Tenochtitlan's Mayor Temple was dedicated to this god and to Tlaloc, the rain god. Thousands of human beings decapitated during the Flower Wars, were sacrificed each year to Huitzilopochtli.

Tezcatlipoca, or Smoking Mirror, was the guardian god of witches and warriors. In the Toltec version he was Quetzalcoatl's evil brother and his opposite. His image appeared for the first time in Chichén Itzá at the onset of the Postclassic period.

THE CALENDAR

For the Maya, time probably stood
above all the deities. The most ancient of
Mesoamerican calendars was the ritual calendar,
originated from the early Zapotec. The Maya
adopted it, associating it with other similarly
important calendars: the solar calendar, the Long
Count, and the moon cycle. Inscriptions and
images reveal how each action depended upon
the flow of time and the movement of the stars.

THE PHILOSOPHY OF TIME

Thanks to the their exceptionally advanced level of mathematical and astronomical knowledge, the Maya were able to develop complex calendrical systems, some of which they inherited from the Olmec and the Zapotec and perfected.

The ritual calendar (also called the Sacred Round), or 260-day cycle, Tzolkin in Maya, consisted of a combination of twenty names of the days with numbers from one to thirteen. This calendar was used for rites and divination, and formed the foundation of the entire system of time reckoning.

The first day of Tzolkin was 1 Imix. 260 days, i.e., twenty thirteen-day periods, had to elapse before the same combination repeated itself. Because the Maya considered days and numbers to be divine, their different combinations could bring luck or ill fortune, thus all decisions that affected the lives of each individual and the community were made accordingly.

In addition to the ritual calendar, the Maya also had a solar calendar (also called "vague year") corresponding to the solar year of 360 days plus 5. The Maya had understood that the solar year was composed of exactly 365.2420 days, and that a periodic correction that entailed exact mathematical calculations was required to correct this error. They were thus able to achieve a more exact result than that of the Gregorian calendar. The solar calendar, which corresponded to the sun's cycle, consisted of 360 days and was divided into eighteen twenty-day periods,

similar to the months of the Gregorian calendar. At the end of each 360-day year, a very short month was added, consisting of five unlucky days, called Uayeb. Thus, they arrived at the following count: 18 x 20 = 360 + 5 = 365.

Each month had a different name. Since the solar calendar had to correspond with the ritual calendar, to write a date the Maya had to indicate the number of each day (according to the ritual cycle), plus the number of the month's position according to the solar calendar. For example: 1 Imix (day) - 5 Pop (month). The 365-day calendar was necessary to set the dates of the various agricultural cycles and the festivals regularly held by the whole community.

This combination of the two calendars created a third basic cycle, the fifty-two–year calendar, also called the Calendar Round, which served as the foundation of Maya chronology and life. Since one calendar was longer than the other, for a date to coincide in both systems 18,980 days had to elapse, which corresponded exactly to fifty-two solar years. In addition to the fifty-two–year cycle, there were two other systems to record dates and calculations that encompassed an even longer period: this was the Long Count, also called Initial Series, and the Short Count.

The Long Count was the primary date that always appeared at the beginning of an inscription, which usually consisted of five parts: *baktun, katun, tun, uinal,* and *kin.* The sixth glyph was the *kin,* that is, the day reached by counting the total number of days recorded at the time of the inscription, beginning from the date the Maya considered analogous to our hypothetical "zero year." They had understood that counting time required an initial point. The Romans began their chronology with a historical event that, according to tradition, corresponded to the day the city of Rome was founded. In modern

A page from the Dresden Codex *illustrates a 260-day ritual calendar subdivided into five fifty-* *two–day periods. The deities illustrated on the page ruled people's fate for each period.*

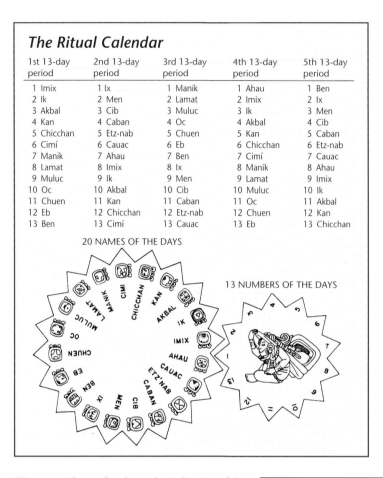

The Ritual Calendar

1st 13-day period	2nd 13-day period	3rd 13-day period	4th 13-day period	5th 13-day period
1 Imix	1 Ix	1 Manik	1 Ahau	1 Ben
2 Ik	2 Men	2 Lamat	2 Imix	2 Ix
3 Akbal	3 Cib	3 Muluc	3 Ik	3 Men
4 Kan	4 Caban	4 Oc	4 Akbal	4 Cib
5 Chicchan	5 Etz-nab	5 Chuen	5 Kan	5 Caban
6 Cimí	6 Cauac	6 Eb	6 Chicchan	6 Etz-nab
7 Manik	7 Ahau	7 Ben	7 Cimí	7 Cauac
8 Lamat	8 Imix	8 Ix	8 Manik	8 Ahau
9 Muluc	9 Ik	9 Men	9 Lamat	9 Imix
10 Oc	10 Akbal	10 Cib	10 Muluc	10 Ik
11 Chuen	11 Kan	11 Caban	11 Oc	11 Akbal
12 Eb	12 Chicchan	12 Etz-nab	12 Chuen	12 Kan
13 Ben	13 Cimí	13 Cauac	13 Eb	13 Chicchan

20 NAMES OF THE DAYS

13 NUMBERS OF THE DAYS

In the 260-day ritual calendar, called Tzolkin, the names of the twenty days making up the calendar were divided into twenty periods of thirteen. The first five are shown in the diagram at left. Each one of these periods was composed of the name of a day and a number, and fell in accordance with the diagram. The ritual calendar is possibly the most ancient calendar in Mesoamerica. Glyphs referring to this calendar have been found in ancient inscriptions at Oaxaca, in the Zapotecan Monte Albán site, and in the Maya ceremonial centers of the late Preclassic period. Every fifty-two years the date coincided with the 360-day solar calendar.

Western culture, the chronological point of departure is a hypothetical "zero year" which corresponds to the day Jesus Christ was born. The specific date the Maya chose as point of departure for the Long Count was 13.0.0.0.0.4 Ahau, 8 Cumku. Though historical and religious meaning of this date is still unknown to us, scholars have calculated that it corresponds to August 2 of the year 3114 B.C. of the Gregorian calendar. According to the same calculations, the era that began on that day was expected to end on December 24 of the year A.D. 2012.

The Short Count was an abbreviation of the other, a less precise calendar used by the Maya especially in later ages. It was, however, in use in the rest of Mesoamerica; it was shortened even more after the conquest. The Short Count has little historical value, for it did not have a point of departure outside of the fifty-two–year cycle and gave less comprehensive dates.

The Fifty-two Year Cycle

A charming illustration from the sixteenth-century Tovar Manuscript of a wheel representing the fifty-two year cycle, obtained from crossing the ritual calendar and the solar calendar days.

KIN

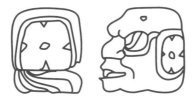

These two glyphs express the word *kin* which means "day," the smallest unit of the Long Count or Initial Series. The Maya used this term also to express "sun."

The word *kin* referred to the smallest unit of the Long Count calendar, also known as the Initial Series. Twenty *kin* formed a *uinal*, which was similar to a month. For the Maya, kin also meant "time" and "sun." The name of the sun god, Kinich Ahau, meant "Sun Lord."

Memorial inscriptions found on stone monuments such as steles and altars, or on temple walls, recorded events with exact dates, based on a sort of "zero year" which for us corresponds to August 2 of 3114 B.C. (for some scholars it is August 11 or August 13, 3114; for others, it is 3113). The choice of such a date, remote even for the Maya, is still a mystery.

In addition to the Long Count, the twenty days of the ritual calendar (the Tzolkin) were also extremely important. Each day was protected by a deity and had a specific religious and esoteric meaning.

Through literary sources such as the sacred text *Chilam Balam* and Diego de Landa's *Relación*, some scholars have identified the guardian gods who, in most cases, are similar to those of the Aztec calendar Tonalpohualli. They probably both originated from the substrate of Preclassic Olmec and Zapotec culture.

The following pages describe each Tzolkin day and their corresponding rituals.

Left: *Like other Long Count units, the* kin *(day) was personified in a monster. The glyph reproduced here is from a Palenque stele whose text commemorates the* dynasty at the time of King Chan Bahlum, son of Pacal. The kin glyph is here associated with that of zero, forming the expression "no day."

Right: *The symbol for the day (kin) in the Long Count appears in the long inscription on Stele 63 from Copán, and is associated with the number zero. The date corresponds to A.D. 435.*

UINAL

The two glyphs on the left indicate the word *uinal,* a twenty-day month according to the Long Count calendar. Thus, twenty kin formed a *uinal,* with the exception of the last month, Uayeb.

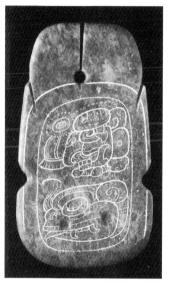

According to the Long Count, a uinal was a month, consisting of twenty *kin.* The Maya of the Classic period preferred to use the word *uinic,* which means "human being," and the word *uinal,* although an ancient word, came into use only in the Postclassic period. Eighteen uinal formed one *tun,* the 360-day year.

In the time sequences in historical inscriptions, the *uinal* comes before the *kin* and follows the *tun.* The solar calendar was based on a 360-day year as well, however, because the numbers did not perfectly coincide with the solar cycle, the Maya established a nineteenth month of only five days.

This month was Uayeb, which in Yucatec means "the sleeping one" or "the remainder of the year." The five days of this month were deemed to be calamitous, and it was advisable not to begin any new activity until the new year.

The characteristics of the solar calendar's eighteen *uinal* are described in the *Chilam Balam.* Diego de Landa gave an abundant description of the rituals and celebrations that took place each month. Each *uinal* was protected by a patron god, whose name glyph generally corresponded with that of an animal or a heavenly body.

In all probability, the Aztec inherited their calendar tradition from the Zapotec and the Maya. They likewise had a solar year subdivided into eighteen twenty-day months. The chronicler Bernardino de Sahagún compiled a list with the name of each month and its initial date, along with the name of the deity to which each month was dedicated.

A uinal *(month) was personified by a human being associated with a zoomorphic being resembling a frog. The refined engraved jadeite stone reproduced above (possibly an amulet to be hung) is inscribed with two decora-tive motifs that are actually calendrical glyphs. The one on top is* tun, *the 360-day year of the Long Count; the lower glyph is* Uinal, *a month from the same calendar. Washington, D.C., Dumbarton Oaks Collection.*

TUN

The glyphs to the left refer to the term used for the Long Count cycle, consisting of 360 *kin*, that is, 360 days, according to a Long Count system.

Tun was the Maya word used to indicate one Long Count year. Each *tun* consisted of eighteen *uinal* (eighteen months), and 360 kin (360 days).

According to the Maya vigesimal reckoning method, twenty *tun* formed a *katun*, which was a 7,200-day calendar period. In turn, twenty *katun* formed a *baktun*, thus 144,000 days. The word *tun* is found as part of the names of all the complex periods that made up the time cycles.

In addition to being used for the Long Count cycle, the literal meaning of *tun* was "stone." The Maya used it to refer to the year because, according to tradition, at the end of each year a stone stele was erected. Tun was also the name given to jade, the most precious stone for the Maya and a symbol of water. In Classic-period inscriptions the word *tun* occurs frequently: *te tun*, "the three stones" or *u tun* or *u lakam tun*, "his great stele," or *uaxactún*, "eight stones."

In the historical inscriptions that narrate the events of cities and kings, the glyph for the word *tun* was used in two ways. In its temporal meaning, it was complemented by an exact number referring to a period of years that defined a certain event. It was also used to refer to the building of a stele or a memorial altar. In the codices and texts of the colonial period, we find many prophecies referring to *tun* and *katun*, usually about impending wars, drought, and famine.

Above: *A long inscription on Copán's Stele 63 contains also the year symbol, tun, for the Long Count,* associated with zero. The inscription also mentions Yax Kuk Mo', the first king of the dynasty.

Bottom right: *Tun personified as a hybrid man-bird monster.*
Top right: *Reproduction of a glyph, part of the inscription on Stele F from Quiriguá. The tun glyph is* accompanied by the zero glyph. This inscription records a calculation relative to the Long Count, followed by another computation also known as the Supplementary Series.

KATUN

The glyphs to the left indicate *katun,* which was the twenty-year cycle, or twenty *tun,* according to the Long Count calendar. Maya rulers built stone monuments to celebrate the end of each *katun.*

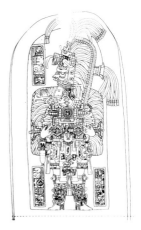

According to the Long Count, Katun was the central measure of time, representing a twenty-*tun* period and 7,200 *kin.* Thus, it corresponded to what the Gregorian calendar defines as a twenty-year period. At the end of each such period, as well as at the end of every year, a monument was dedicated to the occasion.

The term *katun* also referred to the number twenty, the basic unit of the Maya vigesimal system. The literal translation of the term *katun* is "twenty years."

The Katun number is regularly found in stone inscriptions together with the number of *kin, uinal,* and *tun,* to refer to the exact date of each event, starting from a fixed point which corresponded to the year 3114 B.C., the Maya "zero" year. In the city of Uaxactún are some of the earliest monoliths, Steles 18 and 19, in particular, erected to celebrate the end of a *katun.* They show the ruler ready to sacrifice an enemy captured in battle in honor of this date. In Copán, King Yax Pac celebrated the first "end of *katun*" of his life in an unusual manner: he built new temples and restored others. For that special occasion, several unusual astral phenomena also took place, such as a partial solar eclipse and an unusual position of the planet Venus.

Codices and texts from the colonial period report several prophecies about the *katun.* The following passage from *Chilam Balam* reports one such prophecy about the Flower Katun: "The slave brotherhood will disappear from these places. It will be developed in networks, the brotherhood of the slaves of the earth and of the children of their children, young boys, sons of tomorrow's earth. Brothers and child brothers, you must submit yourselves and bear the burden of the coming *katun.*"

Top right: *A drawing of the relief found on Stele 16 in Tikal. The text narrates that this monolith was erected in celebration of a* katun. *For the occasion, King "A" appears richly clothed, carrying a ceremonial scepter and an imposing feathered orna-ment. This type of memorial with inscriptions and dates based on the Long Count has permitted archaeologists to reconstruct a good part of the events of the Maya city-states' reigning dynasties.* **Right:** *A personification of Katun.*

BAKTUN

The *baktun* was a Long Count cycle consisting of twenty *katun*. By multiplying each period by the number twenty, other cycles were formed consisting of hundreds of millions of days.

A period of 20 *katun*, 400 *tun*, and 144,000 *kin* was called a *baktun*. In turn, twenty baktun made up a pictun, a temporal cycle of 2,880,000 *kin*. By continuing to multiply each period by the number twenty, following the Maya reckoning system, other cycles consisting of hundreds of millions of days would result. However, in the written texts that have been decoded so far, only rarely did calculations go beyond the *baktun*.

In Palenque, King Chan Bahlum had a number of steles and altars built and decorated with sculptures to celebrate the end of Katun 9 and Baktun 13. These monuments have been dated to the year A.D. 692. In terms of iconography, the *baktun* was frequently depicted with two Bacab supporting the earth's pillars. Most of Maya history took place in a

Left: Baktun represented as an entire figure. The baktun glyph belongs to the inscription on Stele F at Quiriguá, quoted in the preceding pages. To the baktun symbol is associated that of number nine, consisting of a bar for five and four dots representing the four units. Thus, the glyph means "9 Baktun." Together with the others, it forms a Long Count calendrical character.

four-hundred year span of the tenth *baktun*. However, contrary to what might be reasonable to infer, only the rulers of a few cities—Uaxactún and Oxpemúl among them—celebrated the end of that long cycle.

Twelve years after the beginning of the eleventh baktun, in A.D. 842, the inscriptions on the Pyramid of the High Priest in Chichén Itzá reported an unhappy event: the arrival and ascent to the throne of the Itzá dynasty, a new ruling class considered by the Maya to be a barbaric, hybrid lineage. It was precisely this regular recording during the Classic era of the various Long Count cycles and of events that accompanied them that has allowed us to begin to understand the Maya's mysterious past.

The baktun glyph is associated with number nine also in the first part of the inscription on Stele 63

from Copán. It is preceded by the glyph introducing the month of Ceh.

POP

The glyph to the left refers to the first month of the Maya year, called Pop, according to the solar calendar. The jaguar was the month's guardian, and festivals celebrating the new year took place in this month.

Pop was the first month of the year. All the gods were called upon to protect this precious moment when the New Year ceremonies took place, to which the entire population, without any caste privileges, participated. The guardian animal was the jaguar.

The central, highest ritual was the renewal of all household objects. Each household was scrubbed from top to bottom and tradition required that old, broken utensils be thrown into the city's dump and replaced with new ones.

The population chose four assistants, called *chac,* to assist the priest during the coming year. The priest had the task of preparing numerous incense balls to open the New Year ceremonies, which included all kinds of dances and banquets.

When the Spanish clerics set foot in Yucatán in 1556, that day coincided with July 26 of the Gregorian calendar. At that time, the inaugural days on which the new year could begin were Kan, Muluc, Ix, and Cauac. In earlier times, however, the inaugural days had been different. A cardinal point was associated with each day: the Kan years were coupled with east, the Muluc years with north, the Ix with west, and the Cauac with south.

Each year, similar festivals and rituals took place, which differed only in a few details. Pottery idols were made of various gods depending on the year, and the statues were placed in different parts of the city. The populace sacrificed turkeys, dogs, and other animals to them, and made offers of perfumed incense, maize, and alcoholic beverages such as pulque. During unlucky years afflicted with epidemics, drought, or famine, it was the priests' task to commission more divine effigies and to intensify the rituals, even to the point of performing human sacrifices.

In addition to Diego de Landa's *Relación,* the *Dresden Codex* amply illustrates New Year rituals and ceremonies, with several tables covering the festivities. Some birds, the turkey in particular, took on an important role, along with the quetzal and the hummingbird, since after their sacrifice the priests would read omens and prophecies from their entrails.

In other ancient civilizations, such as the Etruscans in ancient Italy, the augurs, or the priests in charge of these rituals, also sacrificed specific birds in order to read divination from their entrails.

This image is from a page of the Dresden Codex. *It illustrates the complex ceremonies that ushered in the new year. The detail refers to the sacrifice of a turkey. This bird had a particular meaning, like the quetzal bird.*

ZOTZ AND ZEC

The bat was the guardian of the month of Zotz. During Zec, the following month, celebrations were held to honor beekeeping and honey production; the bee god was worshiped.

In the fourth month of the year, called Zotz, beekeepers began preparations for the festivals that were celebrated in honor of beekeeping and honey in the following month of Zec. We have no other details about Zotz, except that the bat was its protector. In *Popol Vuh* this bat, called Camatzotz, lived in the "bat house." This deity was somehow related to death, and the codices portrayed it as a vampire, holding a sacrificial knife in one hand and a victim in the other.

Beekeepers began their ceremonies only at the beginning of Zec: their purpose was to honor the bee god and the four Bacab, one of them especially, Hobnil Bacab, to ensure an abundant production of honey for the coming year. Honey was used to make special propitiatory effigies that were then pressed on incense tablets and burned in the course of the ceremonies. In addition, the festival organizers distributed large quantities of honey to everyone, to ingratiate themselves to the gods. Preferably, honey was mixed with the bark of the *balché* tree, which resulted in a fermented beverage to be drunk in honor of the gods.

Beekeepers held an important place in Maya society for they produced wax, which was used for lighting and for many everyday activities. Honey was a staple food since no other sweetener existed; it was used for all kinds of flat breads and tortillas, and to increase the alcohol level of many beverages.

One historical document which supports the importance of beekeepers is the *Madrid Codex*, which includes a long chapter describing the person in charge of beekeeping and several types of ceremonies he was required to

perform to guard against the danger of beehive disease and the gods' malevolence.

Above: *This lovely polychrome vase is decorated with a painted bat, patron of the month of Zotz, associated with the negative forces of the night and the netherworld.*

Below: *The jester depicted in this vase painting, with the long nose, recalls the merchant and cocoa god.*

MUAN AND PAX

The fifteenth month of the year, Muan, was the month of the cocoa growers. In the following month, Pax, a great collective feast took place in honor of Red Father Puma.

The cocoa growers had as important a place in Maya society as beekeepers, for like honey, cocoa was a basic staple of their economy. In Muan, the fifteenth month of the year, a special ceremony was reserved for this class of growers, dedicated to two gods in particular: Ek Chuah, protector of the cocoa plant and merchants, and Hobnil, one of the four Bacab. The main ritual consisted in sacrificing a dark, spotted-skin dog, whose color recalled that of the brown cocoa beans, fruit of the *Theobroma cacao*. The animal was offered to the gods so that they might be charitable and bless the community with a generous harvest.

Another special ritual consisted in presenting the effigies of the gods with votive offerings, for example, iguanas painted blue and feathers of the same color, which were clear references to water purification. Diego de Landa reported that strangely, unlike other festivities, at the closing banquet of this festival no one was allowed to get drunk, for each participant could only have three glasses of an alcoholic beverage.

A poetic image of the fifteenth month is found in *Chilám Balám*, where it is written: "During the month of Muan, the sun stops its course in the Sky Belt." This quote has been interpreted to refer to the Milky Way.

After Muan and the cocoa festival came the month of Pax, whose patron was a Roman-profiled male deity, possibly one of the ancient gods worshiped as the Palenque Triad.

Although everyone participated, this festival, which took place at precisely this time of the year, was directed primarily to warriors since it was dedicated to Red Father Puma, guardian of victorious battles and wars. Five days before the feast, the war captain who was elected every year, Nacom, was brought to the temple of the main city on a rich palanquin. Once there, incense was burned and he received all kinds of honors. For five days, Red Father Puma was the recipient of votive gifts along with prayers and incense burning and warriors danced a special dance, called Holkan Okot. During the central ceremony the sacrifices, consisting of burning animals on large bonfires, intensified. After the rich banquet, the Nacom was carried in procession around the temple and returned to his dwelling only at the end of the festival.

This lovely painted and stuccoed cylinder vase shows a high-ranking official drinking a bowl of chocolate.

UO AND ZIP

During Uo, the second month of the year, dedicated to ceremonies in honor of the patron gods of hunting and fishing, the priests pronounced oracles. The festival continued in the following month, Zip.

Certain months of the year were dedicated to festivals honoring the patron deities of specific activities such as hunting, fishing, medicine, and witchcraft. The second month of the year, Uo, was dedicated to the patron of number seven. During the central ritual celebrated in the month, the priests consulted sacred texts and pronounced auspices and oracles for the new year. This took place during a ceremony in honor of Itzamná, the month's patron god, worshiped in his manifestation as the Jaguar of the Night Sun. Then a great feast called Okot Uil began, which included a solemn dance and rich banquets where strong alcoholic beverages were served.

Unlike the rituals that ushered in the new year, Uo's celebrations were restricted to four classes of people—hunters, fishermen, medicine men, and witches—each of whom honored their patron god. In the Preclassic and in much of the Classic period, most likely these roles were held

Stone ceremonial scepter from Guatemala, dated to the late Classic period, with a relief of the mythical Maya hero Hun Hunahpu, identified by his name glyph. He is wearing a typical hunter's cap.

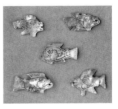

These pretty shell fishes from a tomb in the Chiapas region date to the middle Classic period. New York, William More Collection.

by only one individual, the shaman, who was in charge of divine worship and possessed magic powers, including the power of healing. Over time, the shaman was replaced by individuals with specific tasks, such as priests, who were in charge of worship and sacrifices; medicine men; and magicians. All of these individuals, together with the hunters and the fishermen, continued their celebrations in the following month, Zip. The guardian of Zip was a snake-like deity, whose identity is still unknown.

A drawing of a scene engraved on a decorative bone from Tikal, showing two guardian gods of fishing, one of them wearing a fish trap on the back.

ZAC AND CEH

The month of Zac was dedicated to lesser deities, the protectors of hunting. There are no specific details about the twelfth month, Ceh, except that a ceremony called the New Fire Ceremony was held in that month.

There were two kinds of dances included in the rituals for this month, Chan Tuniah and Chohom. Their purpose was to ingratiate the protecting deities of medicine, hunting, and fishing.

Diego de Landa wrote down the names of the gods invoked by hunters, to whom they sacrificed such wild animals as deer, tapirs, dogs, and birds. They were Acanum, Suhui, and Dzipitabai. Fishermen offered the fruits of the sea to Ah Kak, Ah Cit, and Dzamal Cum. The major gods worshiped as patrons and protectors of the medical and witchcraft sciences were Itzamná and his bride, Ix Chel, in addition to another, lesser known god, Ahau Chamaes.

In addition to the months of Uo and Zip, hunters were also expected to celebrate a special feast during the month of Zac, the eleventh month of the Maya year, in honor of the three lesser deities who protected hunting and wild game.

It was the custom for hunters to bring offerings to these deities and ask forgiveness for the blood shed during hunting. Although this might strike us as strange, unless it was performed at sacrifices, bloodletting was, for the Maya, a serious crime against the gods. Thus, the action of killing or even wounding a deer, parrot, tapir, or other animal hunted for food rather than sacrificial use deserved to be punished. Each year all the hunters had to make amends for this crime. Thus, the ceremonies held in the month of Zac were not as cheerful as those of Uo and Zip, as they were filled with a sense of duty and a desire for repentance.

At the end of this ritual phase, the month of Ceh, the New Fire Month, began, about which no details have survived.

Terracotta tablet from Comalcalco, with a deer engraving. The deer was a prized game animal.

XUL AND YAXKIN

During the month of Xul an important festival took place, the Jester's Feast, in which the whole community participated. The following month, Yaxkin, was a period of rest from social activity. Yaxkin's patron god was the sun.

We have no details about the identity of the patron deity of Xul, the sixth month of the year.

The sixteenth day of the month was set aside for a major festival in which all the people participated. Called Chic Caban, or "Jester's Feast," it was specially dedicated to the god Kukulkan. Before 1441, this event was celebrated throughout all of Yucatán. After the fall of the city of Mayapán, however, the tradition survived only in Maní, capital of the Xiú Maya, though gifts continued to be sent from other provinces, especially standards trimmed with colored feathers.

After several days in which everyone fasted and practiced abstinence, all the city residents and the peasants from the surrounding villages met in Maní at the house of a member of the nobility; there a rich banquet was held. At the end of the banquet the priests, the nobility, the populace, and the jesters went in procession to the temple of Kukulkan. There, after preliminary prayers and exorcisms, standards were raised to the top of the temple, and then broken. The climax of the ritual consisted in the blessing of all the wooden and terra-cotta idols with fire and incense, and in offers of food containing neither salt nor hot peppers. Many faithful remained at the temple for five additional days to pray, fast, and dance. In the mean-

time, jesters went from house to house collecting gifts and reciting comedies.

It was common belief that at the end of the festivities the Kukulkan god would come down from the temple and collect the votive offerings.

Xul was followed by the month of Yaxkin, whose patron was the sun. After the Jester's Feast, this was a period of calm, when people prepared for the rituals that would take place in the following month, Mol. It is interesting to note that among the people of western Mexico, who were always somewhat isolated from the great Mesoamerican civilizations of the Nayarit, the Colima and the Yalisco, it was customary to organize festivals and shows with buffoons and jesters. We have evidence of this in the very lively and realistic earthenware statuettes of jugglers and clowns. In all probability, the Aztec continued this tradition, as evidenced by the reports of colonial chroniclers.

Like the Olmec—to which this find belongs—other Mesoamerican civilizations held frequent festivals enlivened by dancers, comedians, and jesters. The latter were often deformed people or midgets, who were often acrobats and mimes, performing at court and in the streets and bringing cheer to rich and poor alike.

MOL

During the month of Mol, the eighth month of the year, all the people participated in a solemn ceremony with water purification rituals.

There were several months in which solemn ceremonies were held to celebrated the cult of water as well as purification and the Chac god: they were Mol, Chen, and Yax.

During Mol, the eighth month of the year, the ceremony was held on a day that varied from year to year, chosen by the priests after consulting the sacred scriptures. As with all major feasts, the whole population participated.

Diego de Landa gave the name of Olob Zab Kamiax to this ceremony. Most probably, the name is a deformation of a Maya expression meaning "distribution of the color blue." According to his report, priests and faithful prayed and performed preliminary exorcisms at the temple, burning perfumed incense. After that, the central ritual was held, consisting in sprinkling everything with a sacred blue ointment—the color of the Chac god, related to the concept of purifying water. All everyday objects, as well as door jambs, were coated with this ointment to prevent evil spirits from damaging manual chores and coming into the homes. At the end

of the ritual, young boys and girls were hit nine times on their hands by a priest or an old priestess, that they might become proficient workers and craftsmen.

A second ceremony was held during this month, which however could be moved to another time of the year, in case of unfavorable auspices. This was the so-called "making of the gods": all those who were interested could ask woodworking artisans to fashion wooden statues of deities out of cedar. Usually, artisans were unwilling to comply because according to Maya belief, anyone who reproduced the image of a god was liable to attract evil and affliction upon his family. The making of such idols took place among fasting, self-mutilation, and other rituals that continued until all the statues were completed.

Left: *A terra-cotta vessel from the Postclassic period bearing the features of the god Chac, with his prominent snout and a mask over his eyes. The vessel is painted blue, symbol of purifying water.*

Above: *This perforated jade plaque was found in Calakmul and is dated to the late Classic period. Possibly a rattle, it is decorated with incised glyphs. Jade was associated with the cult of fertility, pure water and the god Chac.*

CHEN AND YAX

The month of Chen was under the tutelage of the moon goddess. In Yax, the following month and the tenth of the year, an important ceremony was held in honor of the Chac god and its four aspects, which were associated with the cardinal points.

The ninth month of the year, Chen, was protected by the moon. During this month the making of wooden idols, which had to be completed by the end of the following month, continued.

Whoever had commissioned the idols was also in charge of compensating the artist, the priest and his assistants, called Chac, who had attended to the proper corresponding sacred rituals. Usually compensation was in the form of large amounts of food and pearls. Following this, the wooden effigies were placed under the arbor of the house of the person who had commissioned them: here the priest blessed them and exorcised them against the evil spirits. After this purification ritual, the effigies were wrapped in a cloth, placed in a basket, and returned to the commissioner, who only then became their owner and custodian. This long and complex ceremony ended with a festive banquet where pulque, the fermented beverage made from agave leaves, was consumed.

In the following month, Yax, the entire population participated in a large renewal ceremony dedicated to the god Chac and the four Chac, the other personifications or aspects of the main god, associated with the four corners of the world and the four cardinal points. This feast was called Ocná in Maya, which means "to enter the home."

The four Chac (also known as Bacab) were consulted by soothsayers about the best day in which the ceremony to renew the temple of the rain god should take place. New idols and incense burners were fashioned for this occasion. Depending on the particular situation, sometimes the temple was totally rebuilt, and during the dedication of the new building, a memorial plaque was placed on the temple's walls.

This terra-cotta incense burner is from Mayapán, one of the last Maya strongholds before the Spanish conquest. It represents the god Chac, or a priest of his cult with the traditional mask and the trunk-like nose, and is dated to about A.D. 1200, when the cult of this god and the sacred cenote were still very much alive in Yucatán.

MAC AND KANKIN

During the thirteenth month of the year, Mac, the elders participated in a feast called Tupp Kap, or the "killing of the fire." We have no details concerning the following month, Kankin.

The patron of the month of Mac was a youthful-looking god who has not been identified. At this time of the year, only the elders of the urban centers and the villages celebrated a feast honoring the four Chac and the supreme god, Itzamná. This festival was called Tupp Kap, "killing of the fire."

First, groups of elders organized a large hunt, capturing wild birds and animals of all kinds, to offer them in sacrifice. After the hunt, the ceremony proper began: fagots were thrown into the temple's courtyard and after the usual incense ritual, large bonfires were lit, then the priests tore the heart from the sacrificed animals and threw them into the fire. The priests in charge of worship at the temple of the god Chac, who were themselves called Chac, waited to put out the fires until the hearts were completely burned and shriveled. Only then they did they group in the courtyard, where a stone altar was built with a side staircase: on the lowest step they spread mud, on the other steps, the sacred turquoise ointment. Then the priests invoked Chac and Itzamná by burning incense, praying, and making offerings at the feet of the altar. The ceremony ended as usual with bountiful banquets and abundant alcoholic beverages.

The month of Mac corresponded to the period from March to April of the Gregorian calendar, and preceded the rain season. The Tupp Kap ceremony had the purpose of propitiating the gods so that enough rain would fall, thus ensuring a bountiful maize harvest. According to the *Chilám Balám*, "this is the season when turtles lay their eggs." The month of Mac was followed by Kankin, the fourteenth month of

the calendar, but no information has survived about ceremonies or feasts in this month, nor about its patron deities.

Mesoamerican peoples believed that the heart and its blood were the most important symbols of strength and the best nourishment for the gods. In this ritual, the hearts were purified by throwing them into the fire. The hearts of human beings were also offered to the gods, after sacrificing the victims on stone altars, following Toltec tradition.

Detail from the Madrid Codex *showing the god* Chac in the act of sowing four kernels of corn with the help of a plain spade *of the type still used by Maya people today. The cult of water and fertility was closely connected to all farming activities.*

KAYAB, CUMKU, AND UAYEB

No festivals were held in the months of Kayab (left) and Cumku (center), as everyone waited for the New Year celebrations. The month of Uayeb (right), which lasted only five days, was considered an ill-fated month.

During the months of Kayab and Cumku, respectively the third-to-last and second-to-last months of the year (their patron gods have not been identified), no special ceremonies were held, because people needed to rest after the intense activity of the preceding months, and to prepare physically and spiritually for the New Year celebrations.

All the members of the nobility and the general population gaily took part in rituals whose main purpose was to have fun, eat copiously, and expel the evil spirits by burning pom and copal incense. This series of festivals was called Sabacil Tan.

The ceremonies that prepared for the new year differed, depending on whether the coming year belonged to the Kan, Muluc, Ix, or Cauac group. If the coming year was Kan, a terra-cotta effigy was made of god Kan U Uayeb, who was associated with the color yellow and the cardinal point south. If the year was Muluk, the idol was a representation of god Chac U Uayeb, associated with red and east; if the year was Ix, then the idol was an effigy of Sak U Uayeb, associated with north and the color white. Finally, for a Cauac year, it was the god Ek U Uayeb, associated with west and the color black.

As we already noted, the last month of the year, Uayeb, lasted only five days. As these days were considered to be ill fated, it was advisable to stay at home, waiting for the new year, so as not to arouse the gods' anger or attract evil spirits.

Tripod terra-cotta vase from the early Classic period, with an engraving of a court feast and musicians. In the closing months of the year the nobility burned incense and held banquets in expectation of the solemn New Year festivities.

IMIX

According to the ritual calendar, Imix was the first day of the month. Diego de Landa believed this glyph not only signified the beginning of the calendar, but was also the first symbol of the Maya alphabet. In Maya iconography, it is found frequently engraved on the forehead of God Q, whose Aztec equivalent was Xipe Totec.

This glyph represents Imix, the first day of the ritual calendar. Diego de Landa believed it to be the first glyph of his hypothetical alphabet.

Imix was associated with an earth deity, mother of fertility, and fertilization. It was also associated with the caiman. According to Maya cosmogony, the caiman's back forms the earth's surface, upon which men live. Placed halfway between the Upper World and the netherworld, the earth was conceived and represented as the curved, semispherical back of a caiman or a turtle. Both animals live mainly in water, and it was accordingly believed that the surface of the earth floated on water. In the Aztec calendar, the first day was Cipactli. Like the Mayan day, its zoomorphic symbol was the alligator.

Left: Imix was associated with an earthly deity and the caiman, here shown in relief on a terra-cotta tile.

IK

Ik was the second day of the ritual calendar. Its glyph also expresses the name of the god Chac, who was probably its patron. Ik was dedicated to the wind god, who was considered one manifestation of Kukulkan, and was associated with the wind, understood as "breath," "sigh," "life." This is the meaning expressed in a Copán relief, where the glyph is inscribed upon the image of a torch. According to some interpretations, just as Imix is related to the concept of the life-generating earth, Ik symbolizes the breath that animated human beings, after they were fashioned out of maize.

This glyph represents the second day of the ritual calendar, as well as the god Chac, probably its patron god.

Above, right: Lovely jadeite necklace consisting of thirty-six round pearls, eight cylindrical pearls, and a T-shaped pendant. The same shape is inscribed in the pendant's center and symbolized the day Ik, associated with the cult of wind and the breath of life.

AKBAL

KAN

Akbal, the third day of the ritual calendar, was related to the jaguar god, who represented the sun in its nightly journey in the bowels of the earth, invisible to men. In all probability, the word Akbal means "darkness inside the earth." Several vase paintings contain this glyph in scenes of ritual dances and sacrifices in which supernatural beings and jaguars participated. These rituals were believed to take place in the dark night of the netherworld.

The Aztec name for this god was Calli, which means "house" or "temple." The god was associated with west, the cardinal point of night and death, toward which all men travel at the end of their life. The patron god was Tepeyollotl, worshiped as both Mountain's Heart and Mountain Jaguar. Here again we have the concept of a feline god connected with darkness and the bowels of the earth.

Akbal was the third day of the ritual calendar, and was related to the jaguar god, who represented the sun in its nightly course.

Drawing of a relief showing the entrance to a cave, from a Preclassic Olmec site. The cave opening is shaped like a large, clover-leaf mouth. Images of dens and caves are very ancient.

Kan was the day of "ripe maize" and of the "large flower." In fact, the same glyph was used in the codices to refer both to ripe maize and to Yum Kaax, the benevolent patron goddess of this day, the fourth of the ritual calendar.

The maize plant, its golden ear in particular, was the symbol of nourishment and life. *Kan* also means "yellow," a color associated with south, and also expresses the words "snake" and "earth."

For the Aztec, the fourth day was Quetzpallin, which means "iguana." This reptile, together with other similar reptiles of the lizard family, represented the generating force, and appears as such in the sacred texts of almost all Mesoamerican cultures.

The day of Kan was related to the cardinal point south, which is both warmth and strength, and a special deity whom the Aztec called Huehuecoyotl: "Old Coyote God." This god was worshiped by the Otomí Indians as the patron god of dance and was also associated with the cult of the water's fertility.

Kan was the fourth day, the day of ripe maize, and also of the "large flower." The word kan, or chan in Yucatec Maya, means "snake," "yellow," and "sky."

The young maize god, whose worship was connected with that of the day Kan, holding a small plant. Detail from a Madrid Codex page.

CHICCHAN

CIMI

Chicchan, the fifth day, was symbolized by a serpent god associated with the fertilizing rain. In Maya cosmogony, Chicchan was also the name given to the Cosmic Monster, whose open-jawed

The fifth day of the month was symbolized by a snake-like deity connected with the fertility cult. The name Chicchan was also assigned to the Cosmic Monster.

image often appears in monument engravings. This image, probably of Olmec origin, had mixed snake-like and feline features. It also represented the stylized personification of number nine. These complex snake-feline symbols were also related to the planet Venus as the Morning Star.

The equivalent Aztec day was called Coatl, an exact translation of the Maya word *chan,* which means "snake." This day was related to the cardinal point east and to Chalchiuitlicue, who was the goddess of water and jade, a female aspect of Tlaloc, the rain god, who was her brother or, possibly, her husband. This goddess was depicted in resplendent clothes embroidered with pearls and jewels. She was a very ancient goddess, and evidence of her worship has been found in Teotihuacan.

Thus, the fifth day of the calendar had a complex symbolic meaning that included such ancestral elements as the snake, water, and felines, which in both cultures were closely linked to the concept of fertility and believed to be meeting points between heaven and earth.

The name Cimi, which indicated the sixth day of the calendar, meant "death." Thus its patron god was Yum Cimil, the god of the

Cimi, the name of the sixth day of the ritual calendar, meant "death," and the death god was its patron.

macabre and gruesome aspect of death. Cimi was related to the muan bird and to all nocturnal birds, such as the owl, believed to be evil omens.

The corresponding Aztec deity was Teccitzecatl, "Shell Lord," or "He Who Comes from the Shell," and its cardinal point was north. He was considered the brother—or a male version—of the moon goddess. His image was that of a being rising from a sea snail. According to the most likely theory, the shell was the god's first abode, after which he was metamorphosed from a snail into the moon.

The day Cimi was associated with the mythical muan bird and all night birds, likewise considered unlucky. In Maya iconography the muan bird is often shown with a corn leaf on its head, as in this detail from the Dresden Codex.

MANIK

LAMAT

The seventh day of the ritual calendar was Manik. Buluk Chabtan, god of war and human sacrifice, was its patron. The corresponding deity

The seventh day was Manik, and its patron god was Buluk Chabtan, related to the cult of war and human sacrifices.

for this day manifested itself as a deer. In the Postclassic period, this god was the patron of hunting and hunters.

The deer played an important role in Maya culture. It was a game animal, and according to some evidence, even farm-bred in the late period. The deer is often pictured in codices and the *Popol Vuh*'s creation myths in the context of special sacrifices.

The equivalent Aztec day was Mazatl, which also means "deer." This day was related to the cardinal point west and Tlaloc, the rain god. All three images were symbolically linked to the concept of sacrifice.

The eighth day of the ritual calendar was Lamat, whose patron deity is unknown. This day was associated with a complex cosmogony: the Heavenly Dragon,

Apparently the eighth day, Lamat, was related to a mythological being, the Heavenly Dragon—a monster that symbolized Venus.

which embodied the planet Venus.

Several images in Maya mythology were of monstrous snakes. Usually two-headed, or feline looking, they symbolized the union or link of the heavenly world with the earth. Even Itzamná, the supreme god, was a snake-like deity, and the same image is connected to the figure of Venus. According to tradition, Kukulkan-Quetzalcoatl, the Feathered Serpent, rose to heaven and there metamorphosed into the Morning Star.

For the Aztec, the eighth day was Totchli, which means "rabbit." In addition to the cardinal point south, this day was related to an important deity, Mayahuel, goddess of agave and pulque. This goddess had a very ancient origin, and she once was the patron goddess of agriculture. She appears in the Myth of the Four Hundred Rabbits, a group of protecting deities of pulque, also associated with the constellation of the Pleiades.

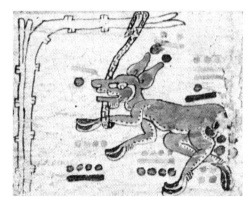

The deer, shown here in a page from the Madrid Codex, *was considered a guardian deity of hunting and hunters. Apparently in the late Postclassic period deer were farm-raised, in addition to being hunted.*

MULUC

OC

Muluc was the ninth day. It was considered the day of the water and jade god, whose name is unknown, who in turn was related to another mythical being, Ah Xoc. Its patron god was Kinich Ahau, "The Sun-Faced One."

In the Aztec calendar, the name of the ninth day was Atl, literally, "water." The corresponding cardinal point was east, and its deity was Xiuhtecuhtli. This was one of the names given to the fire god, who was also the "Turquoise-Stone Lord," which the Otomí people called Otomtecuhtli. Another version of this god was Huehueteotl, the "old god," an ancient deity worshiped in many Mesoamerican regions.

We note here that in the symbols of Muluc there was a correspondence of opposites in the concept of water-turquoise and fire-sun. We should also note that the cult of water and jade was rooted in Preclassic Olmec civilization.

Muluc, the ninth day, was dedicated to the god of water and jade. In the Aztec calendar, the ninth day was Atl, which means "water."

The tenth day, Oc, literally meant "footprint" or "mark." It was the day of the dog, as it was related to a special underworld deity who was charged with accompanying the souls of the dead to Metnal, the kingdom of the afterlife. This being had the appearance of a dog, and recalled the Egyptian Anubis and the Cerberus of Greek mythology.

The Aztec gave the name of Itzcuintli to this day, which in Nahuatl also meant "dog." Related to this day were north and the god of death, Mictlantécuhtli, the most powerful custodian of the netherworld, together with his female version, who was also his bride, Miclantécacihuatl. In the Aztec world, one of the four kingdoms of the afterlife was called Michtlan, and it corresponded to the Mectlan of the Postclassic Maya, its more ancient name being Xibalbá.

Oc in Maya means "footprint" and was believed to be the day of the dog, with specific reference to a mythical dog, custodian of Xibalbá.

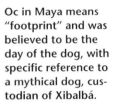

The Oc day was associated with a deity of the netherworld that resembled a dog and who accompanied the deceased.

Ear ornaments in jadeite, possibly symbols of water, to which Muluc was dedi-cated. New York, Museum of the American Indian.

CHUEN

EB

The eleventh day of the ritual calendar was under the protection of Ah Chicum Ek, the North Star god. This day was dedicated to the patron god of scribes, artists, and mathematical calculation, who often took the aspect of a monkey, and at other times was related to the sun.

The day of Chuen was dedicated to the patron god of scribes and mathematicians. This god was usually represented as a monkey.

This is a double figure which appears in Maya iconography as twins with both human and animal features, portrayed in the act of painting, writing, or carving different materials or doing other crafts. In the Aztec calendar, the equivalent day was Ozmatli, which also means "monkey," associated with the west and the flower god, called Xochipilli.

Eb was the twelfth day. It had negative connotations, being associated with an evil deity, bearer of destructive rain and misfortune. It could

The twelfth day was a negative day, associated with an evil god, possibly the negative version of Ix Chel.

be identified with one of the malevolent manifestations of Ix Chel.

For the Aztec, the equivalent day was Malinalli, which apparently did not have Eb's negative connotation. In fact, the Nahuatl word translates the concept of "thorn" or other pointed object used for bloodletting in self-sacrifices. We have already noted how the Maya used agave thorns or stingray spines for this purpose.

Malinalli was related to the south and the Patecatl god, the male version, or groom, of Mayahuel. He was worshiped by the Aztec as the medicine god, his name meaning "He Who Comes from Medicine Country." Some scholars have identified Patecatl with one aspect of Quetzalcoatl, also a patron god of medicine. Together with her groom, Mayahuel was the patron deity of the day Malinalli.

Late Postclassic vase with a monkey dressed as a scribe. The monkey god was the guardian of scribes and mathematicians. The scribes were a restricted, important caste in Maya as well as Aztec society. New Orleans Museum of Art.

BEN

The thirteenth day, Ben, was related to the green maize god, protector of the growing plant before it reaches ripeness. For the Aztec this day was Acatl, which means "reed," which in Nahuatl refers to bamboo reeds, used for building temples and houses.

This glyph refers to the thirteenth day of the ritual calendar, dedicated to the maize god under a special aspect, that of patron god of the unripe plant.

The glyph for the day Acatl was also used to refer to one of the calendar years. Astrologically, the reed was a symbol of power. In fact, a great and wise Toltec king named Ce Acatl Topiltzin was born on the day of One Reed, also called Quetzalcoatl.

This day was related to the cardinal point east and the god Tezcatlipoca, who together with Uhichilopotli was the patron god of war and appears in the Quetzalcoatl myth as the evil brother who usurped the throne.

The Maya often practiced human sacrifice, which intensified in the Postclassic period, probably due to the Toltec, who imposed their customs on them. This detail from the Dres- *den Codex shows a human sacrifice in which the victim, lying on the sacrificial altar, has the heart torn out alive. On top is a vulture, symbol of death and misfortune.*

IX

The fourteenth day was that of the jaguar god, believed to be, like Akbal, a manifestation of the night sun, closely linked to the bowels of the earth and the negative role of sacrificer.

Ix, like the day Akbal, corresponded to the jaguar god in its aspect as a night being and sacrificer.

The Ix symbol for this ritual is clearly painted on a Tikal vase dating to the Preclassic period: the glyph was painted above a snake's head, from whose mouth issues a jaguar. There is a direct link to Aztec culture, for the Aztec name for this day was Ocelotl, which still today is used to refer to the jaguar.

MEN

The fifteenth day of the ritual calendar, Men, was that of the "elderly moon," that is, the waning moon. It could be a reference to Ix Chel, who in the Postclassic age became a moon goddess, depicted as a decrepit, sometimes toothless woman.

The day of Men was dedicated to the moon goddess in her elderly aspect, i.e., the moon's waning phase.

The Aztec equivalent was Cuahutli, which means "the day of the eagle." This day was related to the cardinal point west and to Xipe Totec, also known as Our Skinned Lord, who was guardian of field sowing and of phallic cults. Originally, it was a Mixtec god, called simply Xipe, whose cult was later adopted by the Aztec. This god was customarily depicted wearing a double human skin. The eagle was very important in Aztec mythology: the *Mendoza Codex* narrates that the capital, Tenochtitlan, was established on a site chosen by this bird when it settled on an Indian fig tree.

CIB

This day, Cib, was dedicated to a zoomorphic deity, the bee god—protector of bees, beehives, and all insects. Beekeepers dedicated ceremonies to this god in the month of Zec to ensure a bountiful honey harvest.

The sixteenth day of the ritual calendar was dedicated to the patron deity of bees and beekeepers.

In Nahuatl, the sixteenth day was Cozcacuahutli, or the "day of the vulture." It was related to the south and the goddess Itzapapalotl, also known as Obsidian Butterfly, whose worship was very ancient. She was the patron

A drawing of the Aztec goddess Itzapapalotl, or Obsidian Butterfly, to whom the day of Cozcacuahutli was dedicated.

deity of the stars but was also an agricultural deity, and was depicted in the act of throwing arrows. This female figure represented courage before the enemy.

The vulture—together with the turkey, the quetzal, the owl, the hummingbird, and the parrot—recurs often in Aztec iconography, as well in Maya codices. A bird of prey, it was associated with sacrificial rituals. For example, in the *Dresden Codex* it is depicted in the act of tearing the eyes from victims.

The identity of the elderly goddess often pictured in the codices is still a subject of debate; many scholars have identified her as Lady Rainbow.

CABAN

ETZ-NAB

The fourth to the last day of Tzolkin was dedicated to the moon goddess represented as a young woman, thus as the moon in its waxing phase. The glyph, together with the image of a girl riding a crescent moon, is found in inscriptions from the Classic period.

The fourth to the last day was dedicated to the moon goddess seen in her aspect opposite to that of an elderly woman, i.e., as a young deity representing the moon in its crescent phase.

As we already noted, the image of the young moon goddess was always associated with the rabbit, following a tradition that strangely resembles an ancient Far Eastern custom. Probably the day of Caban referred to this more ancient representation, for which no evidence existed at the time of the Spanish conquest.

For the Aztec, the equivalent day was Ollin, which means "movement." This same glyph indicated the sun's movement, and its image recalls that of a Saint Andrew's Cross. Ollin was associated with east, where the sun rises, and the god Xolotl. This word, in Yucatec Maya, means "dog." For the Toltec and the Aztec, this god had taken on the image and role of one of the sun's aspects, similar to that of the jaguar, as well as the role of Quetzalcoatl's twin or double.

In this last version, the Xolotl god was shown dressed with a breast-plate encrusted with shells and other accessories related to Quetzalcoatl.

Etz-Nab, the third to the last day, has been interpreted as the day of the obsidian blade god, who was in charge of sacrifice and self-mutilation. In addition to thorns and animal spines, the Maya also used sharp flint and obsidian lancets to inflict wounds to trickle purifying blood and to kill sacrificial victims.

This day was dedicated to the obsidian blade god, worshiped by both the Maya and the Aztec. The latter called it Tecpal.

The equivalent Aztec name for this day was Tecpal, which also translates the expression "obsidian knife." This day was related to the north and, like the thirteenth day of Acatl, to the god Tezcatlipoca, Quetzalcoatl's mythical evil brother who dethroned him. This destructive god was feared as the patron god of war, of nocturnal powers, and of human sacrifices.

Tecpal

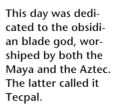

In Aztec culture, Tecpal was a day ruled by a special god, Chalchiuototolin, a green-blue-turquoise version of Tezcatlipoca. This image of Tezcatlipoca, together with the twenty-day Aztec calendar, is from the Feyervary-Mayer Codex, dated to the late Postclassic period.

CAUAC

The next to the last day was Cauac, which in Maya means "stormy." It was related to destructive rain.

The next to the last day of Tzolkin was Cauac, which means "stormy." This was the day of destructive hurricanes and violent storms, in contrast with the benevolent fertilizing rain. The glyph for the word Cauac is part of the name of one of Tikal's rulers, whom archaeologists have named Stormy Sky.

For the Aztec, the equivalent day was Quiahuitl, which also means "rain," and had the same meaning as the Maya calendar day. Its cardinal point was west, from which the devastating storms originated. It was related also to a female deity, Chantico, which means "She Who Watches over the Fire."

Chantico was an ancient deity, patron of the household hearth and also of the heart of the volcano, which hides the eternally smoldering fire that "makes mountains explode." She was also the bride or the female aspect of Huehueteotl—Old God—similar to the Maya's Itzamná, who according to Aztec legend resided at the center of the earth. We can see here that there was an intuition of the inevitable association between two natural catastrophes: hurricanes and volcanic eruptions.

The fire god worshiped in Postclassic Mesoamerica is in reality a more ancient deity that had already been worshiped in the early Classic period in the Mexican center of Teotihuacan. In all probability, this cult was introduced by the Cuicuilco tribes, who migrated there after surviving a terrible volcanic eruption that destroyed their city in A.D. 100.

AHAU

The last day of the ritual calendar was dedicated to Kinich Ahau—Sun Lord—one version of the supreme god, Itzamná.

Ahau was the last day of the ritual calendar. Its patron god was Itzamná and the day was dedicated to "our lord, the sun." Considered a divine being, as Kinich Ahau it was one manifestation of Itzamná, the supreme deity. The glyph for this day means "lord," which was always used as an honorific title before the names of rulers and high priests, in addition to being an appellation of the male gods.

For the Aztec, the equivalent twentieth day was Xochitl, or "flower." The associated cardinal point was the south and its deity, the guardian of flowers, was Xochiquetzal. This deity, as we already noted for the month of Omatl, was the female version of Xochipilli. She was depicted wearing multi-colored clothes decorated with quetzal feathers. In addition to protecting flower cultivation, she was the patron of all the arts and crafts.

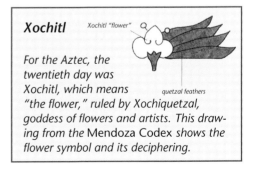

Xochitl

Xochitl "flower"

For the Aztec, the twentieth day was Xochitl, which means "the flower," ruled by Xochiquetzal, goddess of flowers and artists. This drawing from the **Mendoza Codex** shows the flower symbol and its deciphering.

quetzal feathers

ASTRONOMY

In the Maya world, no battle could be fought,
no festival or other activity could be held,
without first consulting the heavens and the stars.
The position of the sun, the moon, the planets,
and the other stars held a central place in the
everyday life and thought of these peoples since
the very dawn of their civilization. Many
buildings that were once believed to be temples
and palaces were in reality observatories.

OBSERVING THE HEAVENS

One of the many peculiarities and unique traits of Maya civilization and culture that still astonishes scholars is the extremely advanced level of their astronomical knowledge.

A prestigious and privileged caste, people of noble stock—probably astronomer-priests—was dedicated to a constant, attentive study of the movements of the celestial bodies, the stars, the eclipses, and other heavenly phenomena. In the world of the Maya, every event was ruled by the movement of the stars and correlated with them, and the calendrical cycles were based on heavenly phenomena.

There was nothing on earth unrelated to the movement of the sun, the cycles of the moon and Venus, and the movement of the stars. Life and death, sacrifice and war, harvesting, or the building of architectural works were totally dependent upon the astronomers' divinations. According to some scholars, even the activity of the artists was interpreted in the light of astronomical considerations. One of the puzzles with which modern scientists are still grappling concerns the technical means the

Maya used to observe and study the skies.

The iconography we see on monuments, in codices, and in paintings fails to reveal the presence of special buildings used as observatories. On the contrary, there are pictures of buildings and instruments used for this purpose in Aztec iconography and in some Mexican codices. According to the more established theories, Caracol, the elegant circular building crowned by a sort of cupola, which was built in Chichén Itzá in the Postclassic period, was one such observatory.

In all likelihood, when the conquistadors reached the Americas in the sixteenth century

The Dresden Codex *is an astronomical work with many tables about the cycle of the planet Venus. In this page the planet is personified as a shining warrior who runs his spear through the turtle god*

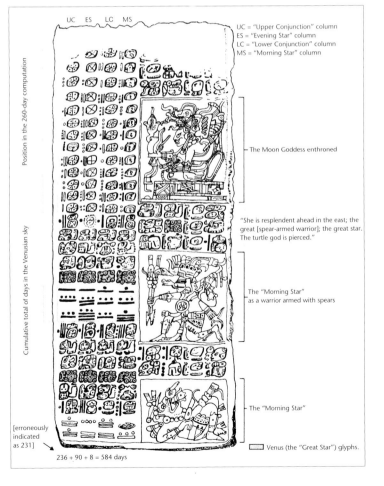

UC = "Upper Conjunction" column
ES = "Evening Star" column
LC = "Lower Conjunction" column
MS = "Morning Star" column

Position in the 260-day computation

Cumulative total of days in the Venusian sky

The Moon Goddess enthroned

"She is resplendent ahead in the east; the great [spear-armed warrior]; the great star. The turtle god is pierced."

The "Morning Star" as a warrior armed with spears

The "Morning Star"

[erroneously indicated as 231]

236 + 90 + 8 = 584 days

Venus (the "Great Star") glyphs.

the Caracol building was still in use as an observatory. In all likelihood also, Maya architects had oriented its windows taking into account the position of the sun, of Venus, of equinoxes, and the cardinal points. In the view of some scholars, the tower in the large Palenque building called the palace was also an observatory. This theory is supported by factors such as its unusual height and atypical structure compared to other ceremonial buildings. Other examples of astronomical observation might be the aligning of steles, such as was detected at Copán, and of monumental groups such as, for example, the E Complex in Uaxactún.

Another unresolved question concerns the origins of the intense, deep-rooted attention the Aztec paid to the astronomical sciences, and whether it was related to the specialized

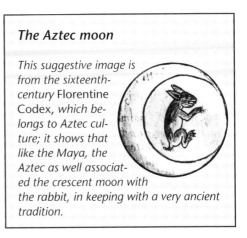

The Aztec moon

This suggestive image is from the sixteenth-century Florentine Codex, *which belongs to Aztec culture; it shows that like the Maya, the Aztec as well associated the crescent moon with the rabbit, in keeping with a very ancient tradition.*

agriculture practiced earlier by the Maya. As we already noted with reference to the calendar, in all likelihood the reasons for this absorption with astronomy reside in the ancient Olmec and Zapotec cultural substrate.

The four surviving codices and the extant stone inscriptions illustrate the role played by the heavenly bodies and all their related phenomena. Unfortunately, the fact that we have no other documents written in original language makes it impossible to conduct an exhaustive research on this subject, therefore, as of today, our knowledge remains quite limited and fragmentary.

From an analysis of the available texts it is clear that the stars were considered divine beings, as was also the case in many ancient European civilizations. Gods were depicted with human traits, such as the moon goddess; with animal features, such as the jaguar, symbol of the sun's nightly journey; or even as monsters, such as the two-headed snake associated with the worship of Venus.

The Creation myths recounted in *Popol Vuh* also refer to stars that are personified and made divine: for example, the stars making up the Pleiades symbolize the fate of the "four hundred youth."

INITIAL SERIES (also includes "18 Cumku")		
Introductory glyph. The variable element at the center is the head of the deity representing the month of Cumku.		
	9 Baktun	17 Katun
	0 Tun	0 Uinal
	0 Kin	13 Ahau (260-day calendar)
	Ninth lord of the netherworld	F glyph (not yet deciphered)
SUPPLEMENTARY SERIES		
	E and D glyphs: the new moon	C glyph: second month of the lunar half-year
	X 3 glyph (not yet deciphered)	B glyph: (not yet deciphered)
	A 9 glyph: the 29-day lunar month	18 Cumku (365-day calendar)

This drawing reproduces the so-called Stele F found in the city of Quiriguá. The text is calendrical and refers to the Initial Series as well as the Supplementary Series. Glyphs of the new moon and the twenty-nine-day lunar month are visible.

EARTH

The earth on which men and women live was considered a surface floating on a primordial sea, or the back of a caiman or a turtle, situated between the Upper World and the netherworld.

The earth was represented as a horizontal band similar to the sea and the sky. For the earth, the band was filled with the stylized spirals of the *kab* glyph, which expresses the word "earth." According to some scholars, the spirals stand for a sort of opening from which the roots of a tree appear, while others believe they allude to an ancestor. Unlike almost all other cosmic elements, the earth's image was never associated with an anthropomorphic or zoomorphic being.

In some narrative contexts, the band is a symbol of the earth, just like the glyph for the word *kab* does not refer to the planet as such—the world on which human beings live, or the celestial body—but rather expresses the concept of territory or dominion. In the inscriptions, we read that many rulers, after waging a war and capturing enemies, could now ex-

pand their kingdom with new *kab*, that is, with the new land they had annexed.

For the Maya, the earth was the middle layer of the three worlds making up the universe. Above it was the Upper World and below it, the Lower World, and it was on the earth that human beings lived, it was the earth that was oriented to the four cardinal points and was crossed by the Central Axis. Sometimes the earth was represented as a floating space on a liquid surface which recalled the waters of the primordial universe, or as a surface that recalled a caiman's back or a turtle shell.

The presence of the gods was perceived not only in the other two worlds, that of the gods and of the souls of the dead, but also in each corner of the living world. The earth and all its parts could take on, or had already, a sacred connotation. For the Maya, the earth was intersected by water-ways: it was rich in lakes, mountains, caves, maize fields, trees, and animals. Although these entities were not deities proper, they could become sacred and come to life through an animal double, the *nahual* of a superior being that allowed it to manifest itself.

The earth was sacred insofar as it protected the maize seed and caused it to sprout, maize being the main nourishment of these peoples. If water was lacking, if the sun burned the plants and there was drought, this meant that humankind had somehow become guilty of some evil act against the gods. To assuage their wrath, men and women had to mix their blood with the now hostile soil. The earth accepted the deceased in its bowels, but also had the capacity of purifying and regenerating them. In dark caves, the initiated could engage in mysterious rituals and speak to the gods. Therefore, man was forever tied to the earth: he lived on it, was subject to the forces of nature and was ruled by the gods.

In Maya culture, the serpent was a symbol of the earth, and in its two-headed manifestation acted as the intermediary that enabled the earth and the heavens to communicate. It was also a symbol of the planet Venus. In the Maya religious universe, there was no specific god or goddess with true human features, whereas the Aztec worshiped the goddess Tlazoltéotl, protector of the earth, of its fertility, and of procreation.

Opposite: *An elegant polychrome vessel with a painted scene from* Popol Vuh. *The mythical twins Hunahpu and Xbalanque are watering a maize plant to resurrect their father, in his manifestation as the god of agriculture. He is seen rising by splitting a turtle shell in half; it is a symbol of the earth's crust.*
Above: *A terra-cotta vase of a man issuing from the mouth of a caiman. The* Maya likened the earth to a turtle shell, also to a caiman's back. Campeche, Museo Regional.
Below, right: *This drawing represents the concept of* kab, *or "earth," which the Maya conceived as a spiraled band. The spirals represent openings from which tree roots appear, possibly a reference to the Cosmic Tree that links the earth of the living to the Upper and Lower Worlds.*
Above: *A drawing of the earth, full of complex symbols, from the relief on Pacal's sarcophagus. The* earth is represented as a female being issuing forth from the earth's crust as a fruit-laden tree.

SUN

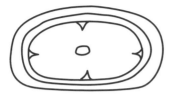

The sun was the star of life and light, one of the highest deities, also worshiped in its nightly journey as a jaguar. Together with Venus, it was the most important star.

For the Maya, as well as the Aztec, the Inca, and innumerable other ancient peoples, the sun was the star of life and light, one of the highest deities men were called to worship and to whom they were required to offer sacrifices. Without the sun, the most dire catastrophes would ensue, the world would end, as had already happened in a previous era, according to the sacred scriptures.

For the Maya the sun god proper was Kinich Ahau, also known as Ah Kinchil, which means "Sun-Eyed Lord." Although he was usually treated as a self-standing figure, this god was probably the incarnation of one manifestation of god Itzamná. Kinich Ahau represented the sun in its daylight journey, which symbolically corresponded to the human life journey, in opposition to the jaguar god, who was the sun of the nightly travels in the depths of the earth. God G 3 of the Palenque Triad was another manifestation of the sun god.

In Aztec cosmogony, the equivalent of Ah Kinchil was Tonatiuh, who resided in the Third Heaven and ruled one of the four paradises. Warriors who were killed in battle had access to the sun's paradise. In pre-Columbian Peru, gold was valued not because of its monetary equivalent value, but because this bright metal represented the "sun's sweat," and was thus impregnated with its light and strength.

Like the Egyptian pharaohs and the Inca kings, many Maya rulers identified with the sun god and demanded to be worshiped as the sun's incarnation on earth. The sun glyph appears often as an element of the proper names of kings. This religious belief is derived from a very ancient substrate, probably of Olmec origin.

The first iconography which refers clearly to the sun, dated to the late Preclassic period, is a four-petaled symbol, since then associated

This imposing cylindrical vessel from Palenque has a rich decoration applied on one side only. The central image is the face of Ah Chinchil or Kinich Ahau, *the sun god, enriched with many decorative motifs, including that of the Heavenly Serpent, whose two-headed body symbolized the heavenly vault.*

with the *kin* glyph, which means "sun" and also "day" in Maya. The Maya used this glyph to refer to the sun until the Spanish conquest. At Cerros, one of the earliest Maya ceremonial centers, the temple had an odd shape. The path the ruler followed to enter the sanctuary during the sacred ceremony went from east to west, reproducing exactly the path of the sun and of Venus. Large stucco masks set on the exterior walls of the temple represented these two aspects of Venus as the Morning Star and the Evening Star, and the two aspects of the sun, at dawn and at sunset.

Scholars have been able to arrive at this interpretation also because they found the *kin* glyph imprinted on the cheeks of such masks, probably symbolizing the sun in its jaguar form. The movement of the two stars, around which all other heavenly bodies revolved, is also captured in the complex symbology of two mythical beings that recur in Maya iconography: the Quadripartite Monster, a type of two-headed dragon, and the Cosmic Monster, usually depicted at the feet of the World Tree.

With the exception of the Maya, scholars studying the ancient peoples of northern Mexico were not able to identify any graphic symbols for the sun before the late Classic period, when it began to be represented as a disc with stylized triangles symbolizing its rays. One of the earliest solar discs was found engraved on the belly of a raised jaguar image on a stele at Nevado de Toluca, dated to the end of the Classic period.

The almost obsessive primacy given to the solar cycle and its double aspect, day and night, was supported by the practice of the ball game, which was widespread throughout all Mesoamerican civilizations. The movement of the large rubber ball and its passage through a ring set into the wall of the ball court reproduced once more the journey of the star, its rising and setting movements.

The practice of decapitating the losing players was related to the same concept. Some in-

Tonatiuh

Tonatiuh was the sun god of the Aztec. His iconography, which dates to the early Preclassic period, has sometimes been found in Toltec cultural areas, such as at Chichén Itzá. In the codices, he is represented with a red body, a headdress of eagle feathers, and a large, beaming sun disc. Central Mexican tribes saw Tonatiuh as a bellicose and aggressive god.

scriptions from the Postclassic period narrate that such players had to die because it was believed they had been lax in their duties, incapable of making the sun rise again.

Maya astronomers had reached an extremely advanced level of knowledge of all the solar phenomena, including eclipses and the sun's position with respect to the moon and the planets. Recently, some astronomers have theorized that the Maya also knew about the complex phenomenon of solar spots and storms, and their influence on men's lives.

MOON

The moon glyph recurs frequently in inscriptions and codices, the moon cycle being central to calendar reckoning. The moon was associated with several divine figures, and its iconography very probably changed over the course of centuries.

In the complex astronomical studies the Maya performed, the most trying calculations were probably those that traced the movement of the moon, which is irregular. In the inscriptions, the dates of the Initial Series were followed by the dates of the Lunar Series, which sometimes included eight glyphs about the satellite's cycle. One of these pointed out the length of the month, whether it was twenty-nine or thirty days, while another glyph gave the age of the moon at the precise historical moment to which the inscription referred.

The Maya were faced every day with the inevitable necessity of relating the solar calendar to the lunar calendar. To solve this problem, as we can infer from passages of the so-called *Prayer Book,* they probably used criteria similar to the Metonic nineteen-year cycle.

In any case, archaeology has shown that, starting from the middle of the fourth century A.D., every astronomical center in the various cities adopted corrections to make the two calendars coincide. In A.D. 649, for their calculations Copán's scientists began to use a formula that consisted in dividing 4,400 days by 149 moons. This method was probably effective, since it was later adopted by all the centers. Thus, these ancient astronomers were able to establish an average length of 29.53020 days for each lunar cycle. Here too the level of precision they reached in their calculations is extraordinary, since we know that the lunar phase consists of exactly 29.53050 days. Seven pages of the *Dresden Codex* illustrate 405 consecutive lunar phases, which extend over a period of approximately thirty-two years and nine months, arranged in sixty-nine groups, during

which the lunar cycles corresponded to the sacred ritual periods.

According to what we mentioned earlier, the moon, like other heavenly bodies, was considered a manifold female goddess, associated above all with fertility. According to both the Maya and the Aztec, the surface of the moon contained the shape of a rabbit.

A detail from a page of the Dresden Codex *showing a deity pictured as a young woman. Some scholars believe it is a personification of the moon,* *although this is debatable. She is shown with several birds on her head, possibly referring to divination.*

SKY

In Maya, the sky was called *chan,* a word that also meant "snake." According to Maya cosmogony, the sky was the abode of the gods and was supported by the Cosmic Tree.

The Maya concept of sky was manifold. This term referred first of all to the highest of the vertical layers into which the Cosmos was divided, i.e., the Upper World: it was the celestial vault, the sacred abode of the gods. The astral phenomena were the subject of deep, ongoing studies. As with the Aztec, the sky was in turn divided into thirteen layers or vertical levels, ruled by thirteen Night Lords.

The Milky Way and the fixed stars formed a kind of canopy in the night sky. The movements of the constellations, the moon, and the planets denoted the regular movements of the gods: any disturbance to this system was bound to cause great harm to human beings. For this reason, a restricted caste of wise men was constantly on the alert exploring the skies, suggesting to rulers and the general populace how and when to do certain things, depending on the location of the stars.

Thus, the earthly world where men lived was connected to the heavenly world through the Cosmic Tree that passed through the world's center. Kings and shamans were allowed to reach this sort of paradise and communicate with the supernatural beings that resided there by means of shamanistic rituals and the Serpent Vision which we covered earlier. It is important to note here that the Maya word *chan* or *kan* also means "snake."

Chan Bahlum, Palenque's ruler, dedicated the Temple of the Cross, and in so doing wanted to repeat symbolically the act his ancestor, God G 1, had performed upon creation. A vase painting illustrates God G 1 as he raises the sky from the primordial waters of the netherworld to the top of the universe, at the same time creating the Cosmic Tree and the Great Cross.

The sky was represented graphically by a horizontal band divided into rectangular spaces by vertical stripes: each space was filled with a star glyph, a planet glyph, or a constellation glyph, most of which have yet to be decoded. This sort of heavenly band was also used to frame images or objects, and even as a border in clothes.

Detail from the Dresden Codex. *The snake is indicated as Chan, which also translated the term "sky" and appears regularly because it is connected to the planet Venus and also the sky's vault. The snake holds a feline in its jaws, probably an ocelot, which also had a special cosmogonic meaning.*

VENUS

For the Maya, this glyph represented the planet Venus, considered a divine star, to be feared because it was a harbinger of war and misfortune. One of the names of Venus was Noh Ek, "Great Star."

We now know that the Maya made precise calculations about the movements of the planet Venus, and that in all likelihood they knew of the existence of Mercury, Mars, Jupiter, and Saturn.

Astronomers had concluded that the Morning Star and the Evening Star were in reality one and the same body, Venus, to which they probably gave two different names: Noh Ek, which means "Great Star," and Xuc Ek, which means "The Wasp Star." The Maya believed that the Venusian synodic revolution corresponded to 584 days. If we consider that the current measurements of this revolution are 583.92 days, we can readily see that their astronomical knowledge had reached an exceptionally advanced level.

Venus's apparent year, i.e., its synodic revolution, is composed of four periods: the first corresponds to the lower conjunction, during which time the star becomes the Morning Star; this period lasts 240 days. The second period corresponds to the upper conjunction, when the star disappears for approximately three months. In the third period we see it as the Evening Star for another 240 days; finally, we have the lower conjunction when the star disappears for another two weeks.

The Maya gave to the Venusian periods values that were slightly different from their real values, however the sum of all the days of the periods was still 584. They had probably adjusted their calculations about Venus to their calculations of the lunar phases, so that five Venus years corresponded to eight solar years. The Maya astronomers were knowledgeable enough to lengthen each year of the Venus cycle by 8/100 of a day, and had even predicted a correcting system which made the system valid for 384 years by juxtaposing three separate Venus calendars.

The tables of these astronomical calculations are extremely complex and interesting, and can be found in the *Dresden Codex* and the recently discovered *Grolier Codex*.

From a mythological point of view, Venus was an important star, and was often associated with war. The glyph that renders the word "war"

One personification of the planet Venus as a "shining warrior from the east," that is, as the Morning Star, from the Dresden Codex. *In Maya religious and mythological* texts, Venus is an important planet, like the sun: its cycle and movements were extensively studied by astronomers, as many pages of the Dresden Codex *make clear.*

consisted of the planet's glyph plus other elements, such as the symbol of the city to be conquered. One example from inscriptions concerns the city of Seibal that was attacked and subdued by two rival cities. The date of this event corresponds to the Gregorian calendar date of June 29, 735. This day had been considered auspicious, because at that specific time Venus was entering its Evening Star phase.

Venus was also important in the mythology of other Mesoamerican populations. According to legend, Quetzalcoatl, the Toltec and Aztec god whom the Maya transformed into Kukulkan, after being expelled from the earth "rose to heaven in flames and became the Morning Star."

There is a passage in *Popol Vuh* about the myth of creation that makes reference to the planet Venus: "There in Tulán Zuivá, the place whence they had come, they fasted continuously while waiting for dawn, and were looking to

see when the sun would rise. They also took turns in observing the great star Icoquih, which rises even before the sun, as the sun is about to rise, bright Icoquih, which was always before them in the east, when they were still in Tulán, the place whence their god came." The name Icoquih, referring to Venus, literally means "She who carries the sun on her shoulders."

Above: *Detail from the famous wall paintings at Cacaxtla, a necropolis from the end of the Classic period. Here, a man-bird is carrying a ceremonial scepter and overlooking a feathered snake, which was connected to the god Kukulkan and the planet Venus.*
Left: *A fragment of the Grolier Codex showing a skeletal image of Venus about to decapitate a prisoner, a good omen before war or a sacrifice.*

MARS AND THE
OTHER PLANETS

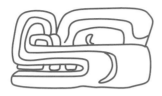

The glyphs for Venus and Mars are the only planet glyphs. However, from computations found in the *Dresden Codex* we know that the Maya were knowledgeable about and studied Jupiter, Mercury, and Saturn.

Today there is general agreement that the Maya were not only knowledgeable about Venus whose movements they had studied with great precision, but also about other planets in the solar system.

One table in the *Dresden Codex* contains a series of numbers, all multiples of 78. Although in the past many scholars, among them Sir John E. Thompson, were skeptical in this regard, it now seems logical to infer that these numbers were calculations about the movement of Mars, whose synodic period, in fact, is 780 days.

It also seems clear that the Maya astronomer-priests were aware of the fact that the number 117, the product of the essential numbers 9 and 13, corresponded to the length of one Mercury year. They were also knowledgeable about the planets Jupiter and Saturn. Recently, some archaeologists were able to identify several references found on stone inscriptions from the Classic period about these planets. The decoding of several historical narratives has led to surprising coincidences: in almost all cases planetary movements and conjunctions affected and conditioned the royal dynasties and their vicissitudes. Additionally, the dedication ceremonies for

Caracol is an elegant circular structure surmounted by a cupola, built in Chichén Itzá between A.D. 800 and 1200 during the city's flourishing age. In all likelihood, it was an astronomical observatory like the Palenque Tower. The Maya regularly studied the stars and knew the movements and cycles of some planets of the solar system.

special religious buildings were always dependent on the movements of the heavens.

A stele in Naranjo has engraved scenes from the life of King Smoking Squirrel. The stele narrates that on June 8, 698, right after the summer solstice, an extremely rare alignment of Jupiter, Venus, Saturn, Mars, and Mercury occurred, and of how the king had taken advantage of this favorable astronomical moment to hold an extremely special ritual, in keeping with the exceptional phenomenon.

The Maya approached astral phenomena with both interest and reverence, since they interpreted them in a supernatural key, as manifestations of the gods.

In the year 690, Chan Bahlum, son of the famous Palenque king Pacal, held a number of rituals lasting four days, to dedicate the three Temples of the Cross. On the first day, July 23, an extraordinary conjunction of Mars, Jupiter, Saturn, and the moon took place, all coming to a particular position with respect to the Scorpio constellation. This phenomenon was interpreted by the priests and the king himself as the conjunction of the ancestral mother, i.e., the moon goddess, and its three sons, identified in the three planets.

An analysis of complex inscriptions found on tablets in the Temple of the Cross has led several scholars to theorize that on that particular occasion, the lords and the people of Palenque treated the three aligned planets as *nahual*, that is, as the spirits of the three Palenque deities. These gods had chosen a unique moment to meet with the *nahual* of their heavenly mother, i.e., the moon.

In other cases,

conjunctions such as these were believed to be actual star wars among the various deities. Stone inscriptions report many other examples of events such as ceremonies, sacrifices, and wars that were closely linked to astral movements of this kind. For the Maya, they were important messages that "those who live in the heavenly Vault gave to human beings."

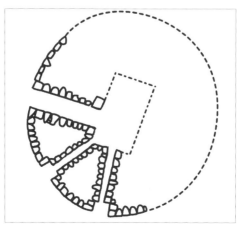

Above: *Detail of the governor's palace in Uxmal. It was built according to exact orientation. From its central door, the astronomer could see Venus rising on the horizon from the top of a pyramid.*
Left: *Caracol plan with the three extant windows oriented according to exact astral positions.*

THE NORTH STAR
AND OTHER STARS

This glyph, whose meaning is still being debated, possibly referred to the North Star, the most important of the stars as it pointed north and guided traveling merchants.

Scholars have yet to settle on a complete picture of the Maya's knowledge of each constellation and each star. Unfortunately, only a few, incomplete documents survive: pages 23 and 24, which are in fragments, of the *Paris Codex* contain what could conceivably be a partial zodiac. It shows part of the sky with three signs, or houses, probably part of a group of thirteen, represented by three animals: a scorpion, a turtle, and a rattlesnake.

Using these and similar images found in other inscriptions, in frescoes and in vase paintings, several theories have been developed. Most likely, the Scorpion corresponded to the constellation by the same name, which includes the bright Antares star. The Turtle has been interpreted as the zoomorphic representation of the Orion constellation, and the snake as a symbol of the Pleiades, also called Tzac, a term which refers precisely to the snake's rattles.

A passage from *Popol Vuh* gives an exact reference to the Pleiades constellation: "Not even one of the 400 youths were saved: they were all killed by Zipacná, son of Vucub Caquix. Thus perished 400 young men, and rumor has it that they became the group of stars which from them took the name of Motz."

Some archaeologists have identified in the murals of Bonampak's tombs, the image of a couple of peccaries copulating. They have interpreted it as a symbol of the Gemini constellation. Although the evidence is rather scant, it suffices to lead scholars to infer that like the ancient populations of the Near East, the Maya had developed a true astrological zodiac.

In central Mexico, the Milky Way was associated with certain specific deities. For example, the Aztec worshiped an elderly goddess, Ilamatecutli, who was portrayed wearing a star-strewn dress. A pre-Aztec god, Mixcoatl, whose name literally means "Cloud Serpent," was apparently identified with the Milky Way's white stripe.

A recent study comparing archaeology and astronomy has yielded interesting results: according to the study, it is possible to interpret all the

Left: *God Ah Chicum Ek, guardian of the North Star, in whose honor merchants and seamen burned perfumed copal incense.*
Opposite, top: *The god Mixcoatl, probably associated with the Milky Way, as he appears in the sixteenth-century* Borgia Codex.

major Maya symbols in an astronomical key. For example, the Cosmic Tree, which in Maya is Wacah Chan, "rising sky," is a representation of the Milky Way when it is visible from the earth in a north-south position. The Maya called the Milky Way Sak Be, the "White Way," or Xibal Be, the "Path of Veneration."

Following this theory, the images of King Pacal engraved on his funeral sarcophagus at Palenque, in reality depict him as he falls down through the Milky Way until he is swallowed into the netherworld by the gaping "mouth" of the earth monster.

From codices and inscriptions, we learn that the best-known and most important star was the North Star, which indicated the north direction. Because of its apparent immobility, especially at the latitudes where Yucatán and Petén are located, and because other stars seemed to revolve around it, this star was treated as a sort of heavenly lighthouse, a central reference point for astronomy and cosmogony. The deity known as God C, whose name recurs in the codices approximately sixty times, was its custodian: his name, Ah Chicum Ek, means "Guiding Star." A beneficial deity, he was worshiped especially by merchants and mariners

who at the end of their journeys would offer idols to it and light large bonfires with scented copal wood in his honor. The North Star god, who was also called Xaman Ek, the "North Star," was sometimes associated with the rain god, especially when referring to the coming winter storms, which were beneficial to agriculture.

Mesoamerican Observatories

The Maya did not leave any images of their astronomical observatories. The drawings to the right are of observatories from Mexican, Mixtec, and Zapotec

codices. From left to right: Nuttal Codex, Selden Codex, and Bodleian Codex. In the Postclassic period, in all likelihood an ancient Mixtec city, Ndisi Nuu ("Clear Observation"), was the seat of an important observatory. Archaeologists theorize that Mound J, a round building in the Zapotec city of Monte Albán, had an analogous function, and that it was especially suited to study the Capella star in the Auriga constellation.

SOLAR ECLIPSE

The eclipse was a phenomenon both studied and feared by the Maya astronomers and the population: in Yucatec it was referred to as *chibil chin*, "the sun's bite," while the moon's eclipse was not feared as much.

Because the solar eclipse glyph recurs frequently in the codices, we know that the Maya were knowledgeable about this phenomenon and believed it was important. Like the cycles of the moon, Venus, and so many other stars, eclipses also inevitably affected historical events. They appeared as divine signs, either lucky or unlucky, according to the interpretation given, suggesting whether it was proper to dedicate monuments, venture into battles, or conduct special rituals on these days. The *Dresden Codex* contains seven pages with a number of tables referring to eclipses. It is a highly precise document, still of interest to today's astronomers. The tables include a cycle of 405 lunar cycles (or 11,960 days). Such calculations were made by multiplying the number of the 260 days of the ritual calendar by 46, thus allowing the Maya to make their religious festivals coincide with the movement of the stars.

The most important discovery about eclipses probably occurred in the middle of the Classic period, around the year 700. Scientists were able to ascertain that lunar and solar eclipses could occur only during the eighteen days that either preceded or followed the so-called "knot," which was the instant when the moon's trajectory met the sun's apparent trajectory. Based on this calculation, the tables in the *Dresden Codex* reported the exact moment in which the two phenomena were likely to occur: every 173.3 days.

Finally, the Aztec as well had developed a number of theories about solar eclipses. They believed that during the eclipse a star demon, Tzitzimine, came down to earth to devour humanity, and that only a whole series of sacrifices could prevent this danger.

Left: *The symbol for the solar eclipse, found in a table of the* Dresden Codex. *Often, the eclipse was represented as a heavenly snake in the act of biting the sun. Still today, some such groups of Maya as the Yucatec and the Chol believe the eclipse is a battle between sun and moon. Pregnant women could not look at the phenomenon, since the fetus could be born deformed.*

LIFE AND THOUGHT

Using glyphs and iconographies, scholars have
been able to reconstruct, at least partially,
the Maya's relationship to nature, their thoughts,
and some aspects of their lives. Although the
available data is still somewhat sketchy, they do
enable us to understand the complexity of their
cosmogony and the rich knowledge this
great civilization was able to develop
over the centuries.

COSMOS AND EARTH

The deciphered inscriptions have enabled scholars to open a window on the world of the Classic period Maya courts. They were able to give a name to the many kings and queens engraved in stone, to give dates to battles, and to understand at least partially why the tombs and the pyramids were built. However, this concerns only the small, restricted class of rulers. Who were the others? Who were the Maya? What did men and women do?

A stone ax in the form of a monkey head, from the Guatemalan Pacific Coast. Dated to the end of the Classic period, this object reproduces the tools used by pelota players. This ritual sport, also intensely practiced by the Maya, was especially popular among the El Tajín people. Private collection.

What kind of houses did they live in? Unfortunately, apart from the two sacred scriptures, *Popol Vuh* and *Chilám Balám,* and the four codices already mentioned, no other literary work or native chronicles have survived that could inform us about their everyday lives and their way of thinking.

We do have two sources, however, that offer interesting information in this regard, disjointed and incomplete as they are. First, the archaeological finds; secondly, the reports of Spanish authors, primarily Diego de Landa's *Account of the Things of Yucatán.* The bishop wrote his work when he realized, too late,

that Maya culture had interesting aspects, also from the point of view of the arts. Up to then, he had accepted the destruction of countless Maya codices and idols, which he believed were the work of the devil.

In the years in which de Landa wrote down his impressions, at the end of the Postclassic

Scene from a Classic-period vase, the same as in the photograph on the opposite page. The scene has been "unrolled" thanks to a photographic technique, yielding a complete picture of what the ceramist intended to narrate. The figures are complemented by painted glyphs.

period, Maya civilization was already waning, having been subjugated and absorbed by the Toltec, and only traces of the ancient splendor remained. The stories and myths which the natives narrated had been partially deformed and blurred by time; their festival and rituals had probably also changed over time. The society the conquistadors found was patrilinear and women in general had no power or authority.

In contrast, we have a much more comprehensive knowledge of Aztec civilization, for when the Spaniards met them they were at their ultimate splendor. Thus, the conquistadors were able to learn every detail of the life and thought of Moctezuma's subjects.

In the following chapter, we will analyze some glyphs that refer to aspects of everyday life: houses, dance rituals, farming; also, information about plants, animals, and concepts that were important in everyday life and had religious significance.

In the light of today's body of research, incomplete though it may be, it is possible to approach Maya civilization and culture. Nevertheless, we should keep in mind that everything that partook of life—each act, each day, each heavenly phenomenon, each plant, and each animal—was thoroughly permeated with sacred meaning. Religiosity was not limited to temple or shrine worship. It was part and parcel of each act of everyday life, from sowing to dancing. The Godhead was present not only in human-like effigies, but also in animals, water, the earth, the stars, and in each corner of the universe.

Thus, an analysis of each glyph requires that we try to understand in depth its mani-

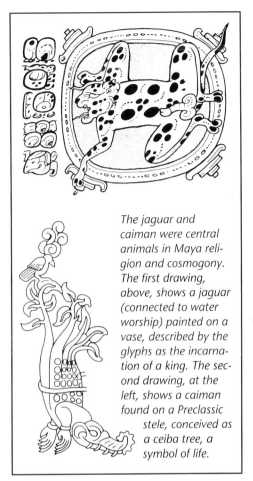

The jaguar and caiman were central animals in Maya religion and cosmogony. The first drawing, above, shows a jaguar (connected to water worship) painted on a vase, described by the glyphs as the incarnation of a king. The second drawing, at the left, shows a caiman found on a Preclassic stele, conceived as a ceiba tree, a symbol of life.

fold interpretations. When we look at the symbol of the serpent, for example, we must not only consider the animal, but also all the other meanings to which this term was connected and their modes of representation. It is a complex view, in many ways alien to contemporary Western conceptions of reality. However, it was shared in its basic forms by all pre-Columbian American cultures, including the earliest and least known of them. Even today, scholars are looking to a remote past for the religious and cosmogonic matrix from which this vision of the world was born.

In all probability, Maya culture took its basic elements from Olmec culture, as well as from the people of Monte Albán and Teotihuacan. This puzzle, full of symbols and gods, is yet still far from being resolved.

COSMIC TREE

The two glyphs to the left refer to the Cosmic Tree. The one on the left translates the Maya term *wacah chan*, "rising sky," which according to some scholars also indicated the Milky Way.

The slab that covers King Pacal's sarcophagus at Palenque shows the king falling from the earth into the netherworld, Xibalbá.

The passage from one world to the other was permitted by a sort of world's axis, the Wacah Chan, which means "six skies" or "rising sky." Two symbols expressed and embodied this concept: the king himself, who bore this truth to his subjects through hallucinatory rituals, and the Cosmic Tree. The Cosmic Tree was the center of the universe, and was usually portrayed as a large cross with complex details. The symbol *té*, which expresses the word "tree," took on a sacred meaning derived from the stylized image of God C. Three bejeweled dragon heads were placed as pendants to the arms of the cross: they stood for the sacrificial liquid, whether blood or plant sap, that flowed from the copal and ceiba trees. At the top was another recurring symbol: the Sacred Bird, a supernatural being linked to the concept of "center" of the Maya universe.

On Palenque's burial slab, the Cosmic Tree seems to sink its roots into the head of another unsettling creature, the Cosmic Monster, also known as the Quadripartite Monster. The Temple of the Foliate Cross in Palenque shows a variant of the Tree of Life. Here, the great cross is imagined as a maize plant, the foundation of life and nourishment for the Maya. Some scholars have identified the Cosmic Tree in the Milky Way.

Cover slab of the sarcophagus where the body of King Pacal was found, in Palenque. The complex relief decoration shows at the center the Cosmic Tree, symbol of the deceased's passage from earthly life to that of Xibalbá, the Maya netherworld. According to some experts, the Cosmic Tree may be read in an astronomical way, its symbolic value being connected to the Milky Way, the great white heavenly road.

SOUL

The soul, the breath of life, was conceived by the Maya as a white flower, to be exhaled at death, when the deceased began his or her journey toward Xibalbá.

The concept of soul recurs frequently in Maya inscriptions. According to their religious beliefs, the soul was life-giving spirit and breath. In some inscriptions, death was described as the instant when a human being exhaled this breath, or when the spirit left him. The soul left the body to travel to Xibalbá. In *Popol Vuh,* the realm of the afterlife was interpreted as a vast surface intersected by rivers of water and blood, peopled by supernatural beings and by ancestors. After an extended period of atonement and purification spent in this mysterious, sometimes unsettling netherworld, the soul was reincarnated on earth. Sacrifices, incense, and prayer rituals could help the deceased's soul enter Xibalbá and face the difficult time of transition. A jade pearl or maize kernel—offering and nourishment for the journey the deceased was about to undertake—was placed in the mouth of even the humblest person at the time of burial.

In some cases, the concept of soul was signified by the glyph of an unusual, highly poetic expression: "white flower." Thus, the moment of death was rendered by expressions such as "his white flower expired" or "the white flower ended." This expression, which puzzled scholars for a long time, originates from the Cosmic Tree iconography. If we carefully examine the bell-shaped objects at the end of the tree's branches, we see that they are white stylized flowers, from which emerge reptilian heads. In further studying this complex Maya cosmogony, scholars reached a plausible interpretation of this image: human souls were cre-

The glyph for "soul" was accompanied by the image of a white flower, which also appears on the branches of the Cosmic Tree.

ated when the Great Father created the Cosmic Tree, and they are the budding flowers of the tree itself.

Tlaloc's Paradise

All Mesoamerican civilizations believed in an otherwordly realm, the Beyond, to which the souls of the deceased had access. This is a detail from a famous fresco in a Teotihuacan tomb; this city was for many centuries the center of worship of Tlaloc, the rain and fertility god. The painting shows "Tlaloc's paradise" with a deity enthroned at the center. The paradise was conceived as an aquatic world that accepted the souls of the warriors.

WATER

This glyph translates a Maya word *sak ha,* which expresses the concept of "clear, transparent water," in opposition to the cenote's dark, murky waters.

Of all natural elements, water was considered the most precious, the purifying element that nourishes the earth and makes maize grow, the element that, like blood, generates fertility and life. Without water there would be drought, and with drought destruction and death. The Maya were obsessed by the fear of drought; for this reason, in the Postclassic period especially, they offered regular, cruel sacrifices to Chac, the rain god.

Like the Olmec, the Maya associated jade with water because of its green color, thus valued it as the most precious of stones, even more prized than silver and gold. This glyph, which signifies clear, transparent water, is contrasted with the glyph for "black water," which denotes the sacred sacrificial well, a murky passage to the underworld.

According to Maya cosmogony, the universe floated on water, which provided access to Xibalbá, the netherworld where cascades and rivers flow.

The Cult of Frogs

Like Peruvian and Colombian peoples, the Aztec worshiped the frog and the toad, associated with water and fertility cults. Among tomb offerings found in Peru and Colombia were many terra-cotta, and well as silver and gold frog and toad figures. Here is a stone toad from the Aztec culture, of unknown provenance. Berlin, Museum für Völkerkunde.

Water was represented by two different types of images: one consisted of horizontal bands filled with water lilies; the other, of bands filled with lines and circle motifs, alternating with small waves and superimposed rectangles—stylized symbols of ponds and canals. There is a close link between these symbols and those of the water lily and the water bird, whose glyphs also translate the concepts of "cistern" and "field irrigation canals."

The worship of water as a divine element related to fertility was also practiced by other pre-Columbian peoples.

Jade, a semi-precious stone, was a symbol of water, life, and a fertility-giving element. This mask, complete with glyphs, was recovered from a Maya tomb, although it was made in Olmec style.

NAB NAL—WATER LILY

This glyph expresses the term *nab nal,* which translates two concepts linked to each other: the first is "stretch of water" or, more generally, a place where water is found. The other expresses the water lily.

This glyph has been attributed different meanings depending on the context in which it occurs, but in any case, all meanings were linked to clear, still water.

More generically, the glyph refers to a place where still water is found, such as a pond, a lake, or a swamp. For the Maya, as for all other people, where this precious natural element existed, life also could be found: it meant that people could raise corn and other plants, build temples for the gods, and homes for men.

The ritual cleansings that were part of many ceremonies were meant to purify the body as well as the soul. Another meaning of this glyph was "water lily," the quintessential aquatic flower that beautifies stretches of water. In Maya cosmogony, the plant element was transformed into a supernatural being with monster features—including heads of animals; fish elements; and a reptilian body, stylized symbol of water—added to the flower.

The canals used for field irrigation were also filled with water lilies, thus the plant became a symbol of the fertility of the earth. According

Left: *Relief of a Maya king elegantly holding a water lily, the aquatic flower that decorates still water ponds.*
Above: *Drawing of a mythological plant-and-animal being, which in Maya cosmogony embodied the concept of water lily as well as of lake, cistern, and canal.*

to some scholars, Maya rulers used a light narcotic substance extracted from this flower, using it much like ancient Egyptians used the lotus flower. This theory, however, is unsubstantiated.

BLACK HOLE

The two glyphs on the left express the same concept: the "black hole place" and the "black water place." They both refer to the cenote, the murky sacred well used for sacrifices, believed to be the entryway to Xibalbá.

In the Yucatán Peninsula, several cenote still provide water in addition to small, secondary rivers. The word *cenote* is a Spanish deformation of the Maya word *dzíonot,* which means "well." Cenote are large, natural wells, the product of karstic phenomena, created by the collapse of a limestone surface layer and resulting in the underground water bed made visible.

Some cenote are over three hundred feet (100 m) in diameter, with depths varying from fifteen to ninety feet (5 to 30 m). To this day, these natural wells are the main water source in many Yucatán regions. Archaeologists have found remains of ancient human settlements around each of these wells.

In ancient Maya script, the well was expressed by a symbol meaning "black hole" or "black water," in contrast to another symbol, "clear water," which indicated purifying, life-giving water. The depth of the well, its murky, unsettling waters, meant for the Maya an underground entryway to the world of the supernatural, which is why they held these wells to be sacred.

Archaeologists have dredged the bottom of several cenote, such as the one at Chichén Itzá, and recovered votive offerings thrown into the well centuries earlier to propitiate Chac, the rain god. Among the objects found were gold and copper discs, masks, jewels, precious jade objects, and earthenware vessels containing incense tablets. They also found skulls and bone fragments, thus corroborating Diego de Landa's reports about the gruesome custom of sacrificing human beings by drowning them in the murky waters of the cenote. Until recently it was believed that only young girls were sacrificed in this manner, though there is now proof that the remains were of human beings of both sexes, even older men and women.

The Bolonchén cenote is an unusual natural well, with the phreatic water layer deep underground. This drawing by Frederick Catherwood shows how the natives had to descend a tall staircase in a rock fissure to reach the water.

MOUNTAIN

This glyph expresses the term "mountain," *uitz* in Maya, the most sacred of natural places, where man could approach the gods.

The mountain was worshiped as a sacred place by many pre-Columbian Peruvian populations, as attested by earthenware objects in the shape of stylized mountains, recovered in ancient tombs. This cult was based on the belief that mountains were the only place where one could climb to heaven, a place of transition that allowed man to approach the gods. The temples of the Moche, imposing pyramidal structures, were meant to recreate artificially an ancestral, remote symbol.

In Mesoamerica, including among the Maya, there was an almost identical religious belief. The Maya expressed the concept of mountain with different glyphs. One of these, the most common, was a stylized representation of a mountain. At least since Olmec times, temples reproduced the shape of mountains and were conceived as the residence of the gods as well as places of worship.

The earliest surviving temple in Mesoamerica, at the Olmec site of La Venta, has an unusual shape: instead of the typical pyramid, it was built with tamped earth with a number of grooves along the surface, possibly to represent a volcano from the Tuxtla region, from which the Olmec probably came.

In some ceremonial centers, including that of Copán, the main entry doors were carved in the shape of an open-mouthed monster known as the "Mouth of the Sacred House." This sort of monstrous mask of a cosmogonic supernatural being served to change the temple into a living mountain. Such an entryway also recalled the caves found on mountain slopes: according to myth, they were the entryway to Xibalbá, the reign of the afterlife. We know that both shamans and kings held hallucinatory rites inside such caves and dens, where they buried the dead as well.

Thus, like water, trees, the sky, and other elements of nature, the Maya believed the mountains also were permeated with a deep supernatural meaning, whose essence led back to the origins of life, the soul, and the gods.

The Aztec Mountain

All ancient pre-Columbian peoples worshiped mountains: summits covered in snow and woods, rocky ranges, and volcanoes were places where man could be closer to the gods and to the heavenly world. The function of the imposing pyramidal temples was to reproduce the concept of mountain as a worship site. This Aztec image shows one of the most revered Aztec mountains: the famous Popoctepetl, a volcano spewing forth flames, whose name originated from a hero of Nahuatl mythology.

TEMPLE

The glyph indicating the temple, *ch'ul na*, designated a place of worship, a house made not for men, but for the gods to use as their sacred residence. Temples were built on top of pyramids.

Several artificial platforms supported the houses of worship of Maya ceremonial centers. The temple proper, the shrine to which only a small number of elite individuals had access, was placed on top of large pyramids and was reachable by long, steep flights of steps. Based on recent research, the most ancient Maya temples are from the Preclassic period and are found in Cerros, Belize, and in Mirador, Guatemala. However, similar structures have been excavated at Olmec sites as well.

As with other ancient civilizations, the shape and structure of temples was not accidental, but was filled with specific symbolic meanings: for it represented the mountain, the ultimate sacred place, where man was allowed to approach the divine Upper World.

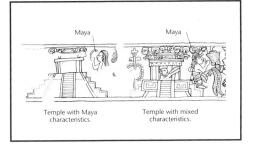

Temple with Maya characteristics.

Temple with mixed characteristics.

This drawing of an image etched on a cylindrical vase shows two temple designs: on the left is a typical Maya design; on the right, a temple with foreign style elements.

Some kings placed their funeral chamber at the base of a pyramid, to sanctify their tomb and give their remains protection under the structure that symbolized the "Great Sacred Mountain." Other pre-Inca Peruvian cultures, such as the Moche, built temples using a similar structure and assigned them a similar meaning. In Maya religion, the square or rectangular pyramidal base was not chosen at random, but had specific cosmogonic references, since the four corners recalled the four cardinal points of the universe.

Only kings and priests were allowed into the temple proper. At the summit of the pyramid, inside the temple, far from human beings and earthly life, they held mysterious rituals that included loss of blood caused by self-mutilation and the use of hallucinogens. They thus fell into a state of trance through which, it was believed, they came into direct contact with the supernatural and the Godhead.

In the Aztec World

This page from the Veitia Codex *from the late-colonial period, written by Hispanic and native artists, shows a drawing of Tenochtitlan's Templo Mayor, the best-known Aztec temple, destroyed by the conquistadors. On top of the pyramid two shrines are visible, respectively dedicated to Huitzilopochtli and Tlaloc. In all pre-Columbian cultures, from the Pre- to the Postclassic periods, temples were pyramidal, and the shrines were located at the top. Madrid, Biblioteca del Real Palacio.*

HOUSE

The glyph representing *na* translates the concept of a house, in the generic sense of dwelling, also as temple, the dwelling of the gods, while *otot* refers to an ordinary house.

During the Classic period, Maya ceremonial centers were scattered urban structures, with residential nuclei built around the administrative and religious buildings. In Maya, two different terms expressed the concept of a house. *Otot,* which implies the idea of ownership, referred to the actual house or home where one lived. The term *na,* on the other hand, meant, more specifically, empty, uninhabited structures such as temples.

The homes of the social elite consisted of large, complex stone palaces built around large courtyards, located in the residential and administrative districts. In Copán these palaces were richly decorated and equipped with several stone benches that probably served as thrones on which the elite sat when they received ambassadors.

Lower-class homes were built outside the aristocratic districts, usually in raised areas to escape flooding. In general, they consisted of five small huts built around a small square. Since these huts were built with perishable materials, they no longer exist and archaeologists have been unable to find any structural remains, as they did for the temples and ceremonial buildings. However, we do have some images of Maya huts, in particular in the sculptures decorating the Labná

Arch and in the wall frescoes of Chichén Itzá.

The traditional hut rested upon a rectangular stone base and had lattice walls filled with clay. The bearing structure consisted of wooden poles that supported a tightly woven reed-and-branch roof. The Chichén Itzá frescoes also show round huts, probably a typical style of that region.

Even now, the Maya population of Yucatán lives in modest huts whose style recalls that of their ancestors. As in ancient times, inside these huts is a small hearth with stone tables for grinding corn and preparing tortillas.

The relief reproductions of huts decorating the Labná arch give an idea of the type of housing prevalent in the Yucatec region in the Postclassic period.

INCENSE BURNER

The Maya word *ch'ahom,* which this glyph indicates, referred to the individual in charge of burning purifying incense during sacred rituals and major civil ceremonies.

Incense was burned at every ceremony. Incense was derived from several types of resin, the most common being copal resin, extracted from the tree by the same name *(Protium copal), pom* in Maya. Sometimes incense extracted from the rubber tree was burned instead of copal incense. Burning copal gives off an intense fragrance that was highly appreciated in rituals; it also served for invoking rain and for household use. In the Americas, as well as in the East, the scent of incense burning had a purifying effect on the physical environment as well as the soul.

Small incense tablets, decorated and painted turquoise, have been dredged from the bottom of Chichén Itzá's sacred cenote. There were priests whose specific role was to prepare fresh incense balls, which they burned inside special earthenware burners decorated with divine images. Bishop Diego de Landa narrates in his *Relación* that whenever the bodies of jaguars or animals were not available for sacrifice, the incense priests fashioned and burned a heart of incense as a symbol of a human heart. Apparently, the Lacandón Maya have continued to observe this ritual in their Yaxchilán and Tulum temples until recently.

Many terra-cotta vessels used for burning incense in solemn ceremonies have been recovered. These photographs show two beautiful examples. The one below, far left, from Palenque, dated to A.D. 600, illustrates a complex mythological scene. The incense burner at near left was found in Tikal. Dated to A.D. 800, it consists of two pieces, and shows a man wearing a bird-shaped headdress sitting on top of a monster.

The purifying fragrance of burned incense was a central part of all kinds of ceremonies and rituals since at least the beginning of the Classic period, whether they were marriages, coronations, funerals, dedications, or hallucinatory rituals.

NAHUAL

The word *uay* expresses a difficult concept, that of spirit, substance, and especially nahual, which is the god's manifestation through an animal.

Nahual is an Aztec word, meaning literally "disguise," and translates a concept that was shared by all pre-Columbian American civilizations and cultures. Its origins hark back to remote shamanistic rituals. In Mesoamerica, nahualism deeply permeated Olmec religion and later Maya religion. Still today, it is the basis of many rituals practiced by some native tribes.

According to nahualism, every deity embodies itself on earth as one or more animals that become the *nahual*, i.e., the god's double. Thus many animals were held to be sacred; for this reason, instead of being depicted realistically, they were shown as disquieting beings with both animal and human features. Even members of the political and religious elite had their own *nahual*, since they were held to be divine.

In its aspect as *nahual*, an animal was not just the earthly equivalent of a certain god or goddess, but its messenger as well, the link that made it possible to contact that particular deity and receive oracles and predictions.

The images on ceramics, frescoes, vases, and reliefs show how the Maya and other American native peoples depicted shamans and kings as they disguised themselves with masks and animal skins in preparation for dances and hallucinatory rituals. Drugs, dancing, and self-induced bloodletting caused them to enter a state of trance. It was at this point that the *nahual* brought them to face the god with whom they wanted to commune. In Mexico, Peru, and Colombia, the most important and prestigious *nahual* was the jaguar. The image of a hybrid human-feline being has been found everywhere in these areas and was a central part of pre-Columbian cults, whose origins still today have yet to be fully explained.

A delicately painted scene from a late Classic vase, showing a shaman meta-morphosing into another being, Uay in Maya, with animal features.

DANCE

Several glyphs have been identified referring to several types of dances, each with a different name, performed by the Maya nobility at festivals and religious ceremonies.

Music and dance were always part of state and religious ceremonies, just like sacrifices, prayers and other rituals. Not only a prerogative of the elite, dance was a pleasant pastime for the common people as well, who danced not just to honor the deities but also to celebrate births and marriages. According to *Popol Vuh,* dance had a divine origin; for this reason, they believed the dance's rhythm to be the earth breathing.

As attested by many elegant, brightly colored vase paintings, dancers performed individually or in a group, and were always decked out in masks, feathers, and jewels, which varied depending on the occasion. One dance of the Maya courts was on tiptoe; this form was very unusual and was not practiced in other Mesoamerican regions. Another dance, discovered only recently, thanks to the decoding of the corresponding glyph, was performed by the nobility, who held live boa constrictors, in their arms. There was also the horrifying dance of young dignitaries who pranced about wildly after ingesting hallucinogenic drugs and piercing their penises, threading them with colored feathers.

Diego de Landa wrote about several types of popular dances in use in the Postclassic period. Usually they were accompanied by religious chants, but there were profane dances as well that narrated epic or historical events. One strange dance was performed by elderly village women, richly dressed and accompanied by dogs.

Chanting and dancing music was produced on different instruments, which were also used by other American peoples. There were woodwinds shaped like panpipes, ocarinas, and whistles made of wood and deer bone, trumpets made of spiral-shaped shells, rattles, and maracas. Most interesting and typical were the various types of drums that produced different sounds according to their materials: wood, terra-cotta, leather, even turtle shells were used. Turtle-shell drums could be either beaten or scraped. Together with the maracas, they provided the background on which the other instruments produced their music.

This polychrome scene painted on a vessel portrays a high-ranking couple about to begin a dance. Every ceremony was accompanied by music, dance, and song. One important dance was performed by nobles who held boa constrictors in their arms.

BALL GAME

The two glyphs on the left refer respectively to the "ball game" and the "ball player." It was not a sport, rather a ritual practice common to all of Mesoamerica.

In all of Mesoamerica, playing ball was not a sport, but a true ritual. A spheristerion, the court where the games were held, was found even at the Olmec site of La Venta, evidence that this ancient practice originated with the Olmec. Proof of this practice was also found in other important centers such as El Tajín and Monte Albán, as well as in all the Maya and Aztec regions. There were different kinds of ball courts: those used by the Maya had two goal rings set into opposite walls, corresponding to midfield.

The game was played by the nobility to resolve territorial claims or marriages, and to hold tournaments. People would bet on the winner. Often, the captain of the losing team

This vase painting, probably from Calakmul, shows two ball players wearing game outfits. Dallas Museum of Art.

The Aztec Ball Game

The ball game, called pelota *by the Spaniards, was played in all major Mesoamerican civilizations. This illustration from the* Codex Borbonicus *shows a game court (also called the spheristerion) in the shape of the letter I, typical of Aztec culture. Unlike earlier times, at the time of Moctezuma the game had acquired a different meaning and had become a sort of game of chance, on whose outcome*

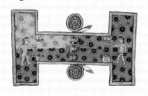

bets were placed, even of the most precious property.

was sacrificed by decapitation; this is what chroniclers reported and this is what can be inferred by analyzing Postclassic paintings. The rules of the game were as follows: two teams of players threw a solid rubber ball into the enemy camp, sometimes throwing it inside a stone ring placed high on the wall. Players could not use hands or feet to touch the ball. The players protected their knees and heads with stiff, heavily padded deer-leather gear, as may be observed from stone copies made by Maya sculptors.

Apparently, this cruel ritual was linked to sun worship, the ball representing the sun. The players were expected never to let the ball fall to the ground, so that sometimes these games lasted several days. The movement of the sun, and the blood that was shed, fertilized the earth and promoted a bountiful harvest.

REAPING, HARVESTING

The glyph for the act of reaping, *ch'am* in Maya, was also used metaphorically to indicate royal and priestly rituals meant to enhance the earth's fertility.

Agriculture was the main form of subsistence for the Maya. Their basic food staple was maize, a plant unknown in Europe before the discovery of the Americas.

According to an ancient belief, maize, a primary element of the myth of creation, was a vital part of human beings and partook of their daily lives. This plant was protected by its own god, and even kings took part in sowing and reaping rituals.

Maize farming in Mesoamerica goes back to at least 2000 B.C. However, a special farming method was developed in the Classic period, which consisted in flooding the fields. This technique, dredged-field farming, consisted in raising the farmland level with layers of fertile mud taken from nearby drainage canals and irrigating the land. The most primitive examples of this type of farming date to 1000 B.C. It became especially popular from A.D. 300 until

Aztec Agriculture

Page 315 of the Florentine Codex *illustrates two farmers removing ears of Indian corn from the plant. As with the Maya and other Mesoamerican cultures,*

maize was the basic food staple. Still today many corn-based dishes, such as tortillas, are part of the national Mexican cuisine. All the subject tribes were required to pay to Tenochtitlan's rulers large quantities of corn as tax.

1000, which corresponded to a period of population expansion in the Maya regions.

Thanks to the practicality of this farming method, all the people of the densely populated Maya lowlands had adequate nourishment. The Maya farmed intensively throughout the year, and in addition to maize, they raised cotton, cocoa, and all kinds of pumpkins and squash, as well as beans.

Wall painting in Chichén Itzá with scenes of everyday life in the Postclassic period, which are also accurate for life in earlier epochs. In addition to fishing and other craft activities, farm work is also visible.

COCOA

The glyph for cocoa, *cacaw* in Maya, has been found on several containers from tombs of dignitaries. They were used for the beverage prepared with the seed of the *Teobroma cacao* plant.

The cocoa plant *(Teobroma cacao)* is indigenous to Central America, where it was cultivated together with maize, beans, squash, and pumpkins. From there it spread especially to the hot, humid regions of Chiapas and Tabasco and the lowlands of Guatemala. The fruit of this plant, similar in shape to a large, dark-brown walnut, was called *cacaw* by the Maya, and *cacahuatl* by the Aztec. The etymology of this word is still a subject of debate today. To the Classic-age Maya, the fruit of the cocoa plant was a precious food staple. It was also widely used as exchange currency in trading, and as a sacred beverage of the gods. Archaeologists have found cocoa beans in dignitaries' tombs, together with other offerings and precious jewels. Among the burial furnishings were elegantly shaped, polychrome terra-cotta vessels. The painted glyphs on them clearly indicate that they were used to drink cocoa. The Maya, the Zapotec, and the Aztec drank cocoa cold. The Spaniards were introduced to this drink through its Nahuatl word, *xocolatl,* which probably meant "bitter water."

This terra-cotta cup was recovered from the funeral offerings of a Classic tomb. On the surface, the glyph for the word cocoa is visible, pointing to its use as a chocolate-drink cup. Brussels, Musées Royaux d'Art et d'Histoire.

To make chocolate, the Maya ground the cocoa beans in a grinder, together with some corn. Then they placed this paste in a container of cold water and beat the mixture, moving it from one container to the other, until it resulted in a dense, frothy paste. The final phase of preparation consisted in sweetening the beverage with vanilla, honey, or hot peppers. According to the Aztec, cocoa beans had a divine origin: the Quetzalcoatl god had brought one bean to the earth and planted it, and Tlaloc had nourished it with Sacred Rain. Once the plant was grown, women learned to prepare the wonderful "bitter water" for banquets.

The Drink of the Gods

Drinking a beverage made from cocoa beans was not only a custom of the Maya nobility but also a practice of the elite classes of other Mesoamerican civilizations. Elegant ceramic "chocolate kettles" were produced by the Mixtec also. This Mixtec vessel, dated to the final centuries before the conquest, is in the shape of a two-headed animal and decorated with geometric motifs. Brussels, Musées Royaux d'Art et d'Histoire.

AGAVE

In addition to maize and cocoa, Maya texts also contain the glyph for agave. The Maya extracted sisal from this plant, as well as pulque, a fermented beverage.

The agave plant belongs to the amaryllids, which includes approximately three hundred different species, all indigenous to the tropical regions of Mexico and neighboring countries. Some species, including the American aloe, were brought to Europe by Spaniards in the seventeenth century, and still today are cultivated as ornamental plants in naturally warm and rocky environments.

The Maya—as well as Mexicans today in many regions of the country—used several types of agave, such as sisal and pulque agave, for many purposes, so that the Spaniards came to call this then-unknown plant the miracle tree.

Pulque agave yields a sugary liquid which, when fermented, becomes the alcoholic bever-

The Agave Goddess

The Aztec worshiped Mayahuel, a guardian deity of the agave plant, whose cult was popular throughout central Mexico. The goddess is represented as an attractive young woman adorned with flowering agave plants. The most ancient representation of Mayahuel is from the early Postclassic period, and is a picture on a rock wall in Ixtapatongon, of probable Toltec influence.

age pulque. According to Bishop Diego de Landa's report, in addition to being consumed in rituals, pulque was used indiscriminately by men and women who drank plenty of it during festivals. Even today, two highly alcoholic beverages, mezcal and tequila, are distilled from pulque.

From the fleshy leaves of the sisal agave the Maya produced sisal, a textile fiber that resembles thick, rough cotton, which the women used to weave ropes, sacks, and mats.

This graceful Jaina-style terra-cotta figurine is of a weaver at the loom. The textile plants used by the Maya were cotton, with which garments for the nobility were made, and agave, used to make rough fabrics.

JAGUAR

This ideographic glyph expresses the jaguar, *balám* in Maya, through the stylized image of the animal's head. The jaguar was believed to be the nahual of kings and shamans.

Above: *Jewel made from a bone jewel, representing a throne in the shape of a two-headed jaguar, a symbol of power and prestige to the Maya. Brussels, Musées Royaux d'Art et d'Histoire.*

Below: *Detail from a relief showing a woman carrying the head of a jaguar, probably an offering to the sun god in its nightly, infernal version.*

The jaguar glyph appears frequently in Maya inscriptions. Sometimes it became part of the proper names of rulers, such as Shield Jaguar and Bird Jaguar. The jaguar was the preeminent nahual of kings and shamans. All the regions of pre-Columbia America practiced the cult of feline animals, its origins lost in the dawn of time. The jaguar, the quintessential totemic animal, was worshiped in the tropical regions, for this is where this feared animal lived.

The images of this feline are more or less realistic, depending on the places and historical periods to which they are dated. Sometimes it was portrayed as a monster, with combined animal and human features. One unsettling representation that has been the subject of intense study shows the jaguar with attributes typical of birds of prey and snakes. One such example are the images found in Chavín de Huantar, in the Peruvian highlands. The Olmec often depicted children with jaguar-like features, and these images are difficult to interpret. For Peru, scholars prefer to talk of feline rather than jaguar worship, because they believe that the ancient Peruvian inhabitants of the Andes were not acquainted with the jaguar, but only with animals from the same family, such as the puma, which can survive in inhospitable mountain habitats.

In all likelihood, the pre-Inca populations received this cult from the Amazon jungle regions, or across the ocean from the Olmec, where images of the jaguar were found from as far back as 2000 B.C. Maya art reproduced this animal under many aspects and in different mediums—paintings, stone engravings, and jewelry made of jade, shell, and bone. Some terra-cotta statuettes portrayed high-ranking individuals seated on jaguar-shaped thrones. Considered to be the embodiment of the sun god in its nightly journey, jaguars were often sacrificed, for their heart was a rich propitiatory offering. The precious spotted skin of the animal was worn by shamans during their magic rituals, by dancers at festivals, and by noble courtiers as a symbol of wealth and military victory.

TURKEY

This syllabic-phonetic glyph means "turkey," *kutz* in Maya, and it appears often in the codices, together with the glyphs of other sacred animals.

Unlike Europeans, Maya and other pre-Columbian populations raised very few species of household animals. On the American continent, oxen as well as sheep, goats, and horses were unknown; they were introduced by the Spanish conquerors. At the dawn of their civilization, the Maya lived primarily on game hunting. At a certain point in their history, they began to domesticate and raise a few wild animals such as the turkey, the dog, and, possibly, the tapir. This practice was also adopted by the Aztec later. According to research and to Diego de Landa's chronicles, the Postclassic Maya also raised deer herds in enclosed areas set aside specifically for this purpose.

The Spaniards were surprised by the

strange appearance of the turkey, a member of the *Meleagrididae* family, which was unknown in Europe. They enjoyed its tasty meat at the banquets given by Moctezuma II. The animal was imported into Europe by the Spaniards beginning in the sixteenth century together with a type of duck, also indigenous to South America. Since then, both turkey and duck have become highly appreciated foods. The Maya valued the turkey not only for its meat and feathers, but also because, as a sacred animal, it was sacrificed during specific ceremonies.

Several stylized images from the *Dresden Codex* and the *Madrid Codex* portray the turkey, sometimes with a rope around its neck or decapitated, always associated with certain symbols and deities. The decoding of the corresponding glyphs has enabled scholars to interpret the positions of the stars and the divinatory rituals linked to the sacrifice of turkeys. *Chilám Balám* stresses the sacred nature of this bird when it describes the cardinal points, since each point was associated with a stone, a ceiba tree, and a turkey, each one of a different color.

Above: *The turkey, frequently illustrated in the codices, was sacrificed during special rituals.*
Left: *A four-legged vase* *from the Classic period, with a cover decorated with a turkey head. Guatemala City, Museo de Arqueología y Etnografía.*

DOG

This syllabic-phonetic glyph refers to the term "dog," *tzul* in Maya. Like the turkey, the quetzal, and the vulture, the dog appears often in codices, also as a sacrificial victim.

Like the turkey, the dog is often portrayed on Maya pottery. As in Europe, the Maya domesticated the dog as a household and hunting animal. They also raised and fattened some dog species for the specific purpose of eating their meat, in accordance with an ancient Mesoamerican custom. This has been attested by Spanish chroniclers and by several pottery finds, which portray particularly obese dogs.

Remains of dogs were found in many tombs of high-ranking dignitaries from the Postclassic era, as were rich funeral offerings and the remains of other sacrificial victims. According to some scholars, this faithful friend and protector had to die with his master to accompany him to Xibalbá. According to another interpretation, the dog was supposed to nourish its master with its meat.

Dogs were sacrificed during special festivals and religious ceremonies that were still being held during the Postclassic age and were minutely described by Diego de Landa. During the month of Muan, the cocoa growers held rituals in honor of Ek Chuah, the god of merchants and the cocoa plant. After the ritual incense burning, they sacrificed a spotted-skin dog, dark brown like the cocoa beans, for its death was believed to propitiate the god for future harvests.

Maya mythology included a being with doglike features whose task was to guard the entrance to Xibalbá, the realm of the afterlife, much like Cerberus, the dog of Greek mythology. Additionally, there are images of dogs in the codices linked with specific deities.

The dog was important to other Mesoamerican civilizations as well, especially the populations of Oaxaca, Veracruz, and western Mexico, the Colima in particular. As we already mentioned, Mesoamerican peoples had very few domesticated animals, and for the most part ate wild game they hunted with great skill.

A terra-cotta figure of a dog's head with open jaws, from a Copán tomb.. The fangs and teeth are finished in great detail and the throat was painted red with cinnabar. Sometimes dogs were sacrificed so they could accompany their deceased masters in the journey to Xibalbá.

HUMMINGBIRD

This glyph represents a stylized hummingbird, also known as fly bird. Worshiped by the Maya and the Aztec, it was sought for its splendid plumage.

The hummingbird is native to the American continent. The Spaniards called the bird *colibrì*, a name that was already in use in the Caribbean islands. They also called it fly bird because of its minuscule size.

There are several types of hummingbirds, the smallest of all being the Helen, or Cuba Sunsun hummingbird. Some species, especially those from the tropical regions, have splendidly colored plumage. Among these, the best known are the Costa, the red-throated, and the *splendente* hummingbird, which are found in Colombia and Patagonia and are highly valued for their metallic, blue-green feathers.

The Maya hunted these tiny birds, as well as several species of the Ara parrot, the quetzal, and other birds, for their highly valued feathers that went to trim the dresses and accessories of the elite. The Inca and other pre-Inca civilizations of Peru shared this tradition from time immemorial, as attested by archaeological finds. The geographic and cultural matrix of these customs, however, is the Amazon forest, the natural habitat of countless species of tropical birds.

Like many other animals, the hummingbird is treated as a mythical bird in Maya sacred scriptures. In the Aztec tradition, some deities were linked to different colored hummingbirds. The Aztec believed that the soul of a warrior who fell in battle became a hummingbird. The image of this tiny bird has even been reproduced in one of the immense desert geoglyphs created by the Nazca people. Thus, its religious importance was common to many areas of South America and Mesoamerica.

The hummingbird was present in the early Postclassic age in Chichén Itzá, in the context of human sacrifices. An engraving in the Temple of the Jaguars depicts it pecking at the head of a man emerging from a flower. It has been established that in the Postclassic age, throughout all of central Mexico's geographic and cultural area, both the hummingbird and the flower were symbols linked to the concept of blood and self-sacrifice.

The main Aztec tribal god, a deity with unusually cruel features, was Huitzilopochtli, whose name means "the southern hummingbird" or "the hummingbird on the left."

The Peruvian World

Along the southern coast of Peru, enormous geometric and zoomorphic drawings were traced on the desert surface of the Ingenio Pampa. Many scholars attribute these "geoglyphs" to the Nazca culture (third century B.C. to seventh century A.D.). They are so vast that they can be seen in their fullness only from a high altitude. This photo shows a hummingbird geoglyph. The hummingbird was considered a totemic animal in Peru, as well. Possibly, these geoglyphs formed a large map of the stars.

SHELL

Shells were precious objects for the Maya, who used them to make jewelry and to fashion musical instruments. They were also a symbol of water, of zero, and of some deities as well.

Shells had many uses in the Maya world. First, the image of a stylized shell was used to express the number zero. The large, red *Spondylus* (thorny shell), common to the warm tropical seas, was especially valued.

Shells were used primarily as exchange currency, along with jade, feathers, and cocoa beans. These precious objects were given to the rulers as tributes and to the gods as offerings. They were also used to extinguish criminal penalties. The Spaniards noted that at the time of the conquest the Aztec rulers demanded a yearly tax of 1,600 *Spondylus* shells from the subject tribes who lived along the coast.

These objects had a high intrinsic value, also due to the fact the Maya used neither gold nor copper, which became known and appreciated only in the Postclassic period.

Shells were used mostly for decoration. Bracelets, necklaces, and ear pendants made of shell were found among the funeral furnishings of high-level dignitaries. Shells were also used with jade and turquoise to produce exquisite inlays for decorating clothes, mats, and headdresses. Reliefs from steles show that small shells were sown into clothing, probably producing a castanet-like sound when the wearer moved.

Shells were also used as musical instruments. This was also true of other pre-Columbian cultures. The *strombus,* a spiral-shaped shell, which produced an unusual sound resembling that of a trumpet, was especially valued as a musical instrument.

Conch players blowing into their shells are visible in paintings and reliefs. People were in the custom of dancing at court, as well as in the squares and in the streets during festivals, to the sound of music made by conches, flutes, drums, and other instruments. According to the *Popol Vuh,* music was a sacred gift of the gods to men.

This refined, painted terra-cotta vase shows a figure, probably a god, emerging from a shell. It might be Puhatun, also known as God N, who is usually shown holding a seashell or a turtle shell.

SERPENT

This ideographic glyph represents the stylized head of a serpent. The Maya word for snake was kan or chan, depending on the geographic region, and also expressed "sky."

Four animals indigenous to the Mesoamerican and Amazonian natural ecosystem and imbued with special religious meanings recur frequently in pre-Columbian iconography. They are the jaguar, the bird of prey, the caiman, and the serpent. Endowed with supernatural attributes, these animals took on the fantastic shapes of dragons or monsters, and only rarely were they portrayed realistically.

Several species of poisonous snakes, such as the coral snake and the rattle snake as well as species such as the boa constrictor are still found today in the tropical forests of Mexico and Guatemala.

Already Preclassic Maya iconography portrayed this fearful, dangerous reptile as a mythical being of the manifold manifestations, whose cosmogonic meaning was linked to the sky, especially when it was represented as a two-headed snake. Based on iconographic and archaeological finds, scholars have established that in the Classic period a scepter in the shape of a two-headed snake was a symbol of power of Maya rulers. The "snake vision," made possible during hallucinations, was the means of communicating with the supernatural world, a link between the human and the divine.

The images and engravings that depict this ceremony show a bearded snake deco-rated with feathers and jewels, all attributes that endowed it with supernatural powers. In the Postclassic period the feathered snake became Kukulkan, a god whose cult was introduced to the Maya by people coming from the north, possibly an extremely remote cult to which even very early peoples had dedicated temples and sculptures. The Toltec gave the name of Quetzalcoatl to this god, which means "Feathered Snake." It was still worshiped by the Aztec at the time of the conquest.

Some of the most beautiful representations of the Feathered Snake are the wall paintings at the Cacaxtla archaeological site in central Mexico, dated to the end of the Classic period, which show this mythical being engaged in battle with a creature with human and feline features.

Snake worship, together with the worship of the other animals mentioned above, was common in all of pre-Columbian America since the earliest times. The extremely ancient archaeological site of Chavín de Huantar, in Peru, also has images of a supernatural being with combined snake, feline, and bird features.

Detail from the Tro-Cortesianus Codex, *also known as the* Madrid Codex, *showing a serpent, an animal associated with many complex symbolisms. Madrid, Museo de Historia y Arqueología.*

WRITING SYSTEMS OF THE NEW WORLD

"The hieroglyphics found on American buildings are too few to authorize us to draw firm conclusions. A comparison with those of the *Dresden Codex,* which probably originated from the same region (Palenque), with those from the Xochicalco monuments and with the more primitive Aztec pictographic script, does not lead us to conclude that there was any system common to them."

William Prescott, New York, 1843.

WRITING SYSTEMS OF THE NEW CONTINENT

The deciphering and study of Maya writing has contributed to fuel a growing interest among scholars for the writings used by other pre-Columbian cultures, for some of these peoples did develop written language forms. Some of these languages, such as the Olmec, have yet to be deciphered. Thanks to recent studies, other languages, such as the symbols used by the Aztec in Mexico and the Inca in Peru, are beginning to yield their secrets. In this chapter, we will present the most recent theories on the subject, staying on the side of caution since these are still critical, highly debatable subjects.

MESOAMERICAN WRITINGS

Mesoamerican writings have been classified into two major categories: the first includes the scripts used by the Zapotec and the Mixtec, from which apparently the Aztec script is derived. The second is that of the Isthmus and Maya scripts. Scholars do concur that there is a strong resemblance between the two categories, which has been explained by their common Olmec matrix in the geographic area of the Gulf of Mexico.

Very little evidence of writing from the ear-

The Monte Albán archaeological site in the region of Oaxaca, Mexico, saw the flourishing of the Zapotec culture beginning with the Classic period. Based on recent studies, the script from Oaxaca, which has yet to be deciphered, and the Zapotec ritual calendar computations are the most ancient in Mesoamerica.

ly or middle Preclassic period, the time stretching from 1200 to 400 B.C., has been found. These consist of engraved symbols, which some scholars consider true glyphs, as well as the footprint found on the Ambassador's Monument at the Olmec site of La Venta, whose meaning has yet to be satisfactorily explained.

Scholars have been able to establish that a ritual calendar and inscriptions already existed around 500 B.C. in the region of Oaxaca, and approximately 400 years later in the Isthmus region. This provides sound evidence that a date element was always included in every Mesoamerican text, from the time in which written script was adopted until the time of the conquest.

The city of Monte Albán is believed to have been the capital of Zapotec civilization between 300 B.C. and 800 A.D. This prestigious archaeological site has yielded a great number of engraved and carved stones. However, efforts to decode the symbols have not yet been successful. Today, Zapotec is considered the most ancient form of a true, proper writing system

The Olmec

This green stone statuette of a man holding a child from Las Limas, Veracruz, is a classic example of Olmec art from the first millennium B.C. It is difficult to formulate theories about Olmec Preclassic script.

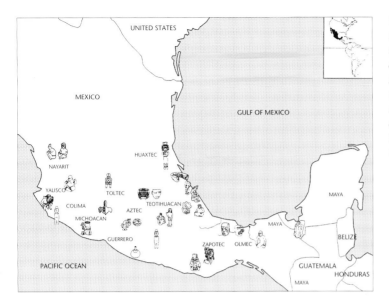

This map shows the location and distribution of the main Mesoamerican cultures. Until now, it has been determined that the Oaxaca, Zapotec, and Mixtec used writing, in addition to the Maya and the Aztec of the state of Veracruz.

in the Mesoamerican area. Like Maya script, it may be classified as a "mixed" writing, consisting of logograms as well as phonetic-syllabic signs, the latter being more appropriate to the morphology of the Zapotec language. Scholars have succeeded in deciphering the symbols for the twenty days of the 260-day calendar. Additionally, about eighty glyphs have also been identified—but only the meanings for a few.

One of the more famous finds of Monte Albán is the Danzantes platform, a large relief portraying beheaded and mutilated men, in all probability war prisoners. The symbols engraved next to the stone figures probably refer to the names of these prisoners and of the subjected cities. Scholars have theorized that many of these engraved inscriptions found on steles had an historical purpose, like the Maya inscriptions that glorified the exploits of reigning dynasties, while others had a ritual purpose. Accord-

ing to a recent hypothesis, the names of dignitaries were more precisely indicated by adding their date of birth next to them.

The Zapotec script was widely used beyond the territorial boundaries of central Oaxaca as well. It has been found in Nuine, in northern Oaxaca; in Xochicalco in the state of Morelos; in Cacaxtla; and possibly even in Teotihuacan, although the reasons for such a widespread dissemination have yet to be explained.

The Zapotec script was fundamental particularly for the development of the Postclassic Mixtec script. There are several ex-

Stone steles found at the Monte Albán site. The carvings are Zapotec symbols. Their writing system, similar to that of the Maya, included numerical and calendrical symbols. Although intense epigraphic work is under way, most of these glyphs have yet to be deciphered.

tant Mixtec codices, richly painted on deerskin, dated to between A.D. 1200 and 1521. These manuscripts for the most part relate historical matters and dynastic accomplishments. Three of them, however, deal with mythological and religious subjects. Of these, the first is the *Vindobonensis Codex,*

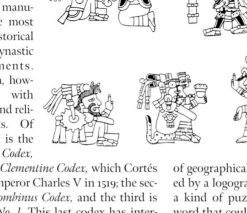

also known as *Clementine Codex,* which Cortés delivered to Emperor Charles V in 1519; the second is the *Colombinus Codex,* and the third is *Becker Codex No. 1.* This last codex has interesting illustrations of religious ceremonies and ritual games.

These Mixtec documents are important particularly for their illustrations, for possibly for these people script was secondary to images, consisting mostly in dates, proper names and place names. As in the Zapotec texts, each individual was indicated by his date of birth according to the 260-day calendar, as well as a nickname expressed by a logographic symbol.

For example, one famous Mixtec king is known as 8 Deer Jaguar Claw. Here the first sign that expresses the name of the day of his birth, is flanked by a second sign representing a stylized feline claw. More difficult to interpret are the names of geographical places. These could be indicated by a logographic sign, though often also by a kind of puzzle, in which the symbol of a word that could be translated as an image was sometimes used in place of a word that was more difficult to express. For example, a place called the Turquoise Hill was expressed by a pictogram showing a stylized hill with a turquoise at its center. Another example is the word "plain," *yodzo* in Mixtec, written using a logogram which depicted a bunch of feathers, for the word *yodzo* also meant "large feather." Scholars have developed interesting theories about the Zapotec and Mixtec scripts, however until they are all decoded, many doubts remain unresolved.

Left: *The Mixtec, who settled in the Oaxaca region in the Postclassic period, adopted a pictographic type of writing. One page of the* Vindobonensis Codex *made of deerskin, decorated with symbols and images, narrates the dynastic stories of their reigning families.*
Above: *Drawings of the major deities from the Mixtec codices.*

The very few surviving texts of the so-called "Isthmus writings" are one of the more interesting puzzles in the field of researching the evolution of Mesoamerican pre-Columbian languages and writings.

In 1988, a large stone stele was discovered by accident in the Mexican state of Veracruz. Its surface was decorated with a relief showing a high-ranking individual in a vertical position. This stele was named La Mojarra, after the name of the village near the site where it was found.

Around the relief are twenty-one vertical columns, filled with 465 engraved glyphs; more glyphs are engraved on the king's body. This is one of the longest inscriptions found in the Mesoamerican area to date. The type of script is highly refined and recalls in some aspects that of the Maya and the few surviving traces of Olmec script. Like them, it is a mixedsystem—phonetic and logo-syllabic—but it is neither Maya nor Olmec. Thus, we have a new puzzle.

At the time of the discovery, scholars had only one other example of similar glyphs: those engraved on a small nephrite statuette depicting a shaman figure wearing a duck mask, found at Tuxtla, forty miles (65 km) from the La Mojarra site.

The linguist Terrence Kaufman and the anthropologist John Justeson were the first to attempt the decoding of this stele. Several years after its discovery they succeeded, at least partially, in explaining the puzzle by using three fundamental elements: some aspects of Maya hieroglyphs, a hypothetical early language of proto-Zoque stock from which contemporary Indian languages are derived and, as a point of comparison, the symbols of the Tuxtla statuette.

According to their research, the text narrates the actions of the Lord of the Mountain Harvest, a powerful warrior-king who ruled in the second century A.D., and the rituals he performed together with a shaman, who was the same shaman of the nephrite statuette. An important element of this discovery was the identification of the ancient language used on the La Mojarra stele as a probable direct descendant of Olmec.

AZTEC SCRIPT

Like the Maya and the Mixtec, in order to hand down their written messages to posterity the Aztec used codices made of agave-fiber strips or deerskin. They were written on both

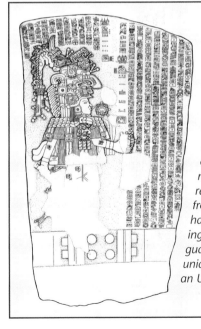

La Mojarra Stele

The La Mojarra Stele and the Tuxtla statuette are important finds from the state of Veracruz that contain traces of a script from the Preclassic period, with a structure similar to that of the Maya script, but expressing a language of different stock, close to the Olmec. After much laborious work and research, two scholars from the United States have succeeded in decoding the texts of this language, which is possibly unique for its kind, from an Ur-Olmec culture.

sides, folded accordion-style, and kept inside a wooden or leather cover.

Unlike Maya documents that were almost totally destroyed, several Aztec codices are extant: some of these, such as the *Codex Borbonicus,* are datable to the Postclassic period. Others, such as the *Vatican Codex,* were written after the conquest by Mexican scribes who availed themselves of pre-Columbian sources. Still others, such as the *Borgia Codex,* originate from areas that in all likelihood had a Mixtec culture, though with Aztec influence, although this is still a subject of debate. These texts have beautiful illustrations and cover religious and mythological themes. The Aztec scribes belonged to a special caste of artists, called *tlacuilo,* which means "he who writes by painting."

Following a long, protracted research lasting several years, Joaquim Galarza, a Mexican archaeologist, has succeeded in decoding a large part of the Aztec script, which is very different from the ones we have reviewed so far. The method Galarza used was to complement the analysis of pictographic manuscripts with the study of the ancient Nahuatl language spoken by the Aztec, and which is still spoken by some native groups in Mexico.

Initially, the decoding method Galarza applied to the *Mendoza Codex* consisted in a complex deconstruction of the painted images into their building blocks: thus, he was able to show that these illustrations made up a true text. The *Mendoza Codex* is a pictographic manuscript consisting of seventy-two European-type sheets of paper, written by order of the first viceroy of

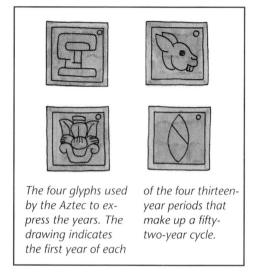

The four glyphs used by the Aztec to express the years. The drawing indicates the first year of each of the four thirteen-year periods that make up a fifty-two-year cycle.

New Spain, Antonio de Mendoza, in the early part of the sixteenth century, using three ancient manuscripts as sources.

Galarza's first attempt at decoding the text was by analyzing the first page of the codex, followed by an analysis of the succeeding pages. Galarza's research shows that the *tlacuilo* had to organize his work following a rigid structure in order to transcribe the language,

The famous Piedra del Sol (sun stone) is a monolith over nine feet (3 m) in diameter on which the Aztec calendar is inscribed using complex cosmogonic symbols.

i.e., in order to express in writing the word's sounds.

As a matter of fact, Aztec glyphs could be read in three ways: ideographically, when they graphically expressed a concept or a symbolic value; phonetically, when they expressed a sound, especially the sound of the first syllable radical; and pictographically, when they reproduced a word through a stylized image, like a true painted drawing.

In Aztec texts, colors were an important element of writing, since in addition to being decorative, each color corresponded to a different sound. Thus, different colors could be read in different ways.

Aztec scribes used different types of connectors or binding elements: signs such as lines, or methods such as "gluing" glyphs together,

The first page of the Mendoza Codex, which illustrates an Aztec code that contains the key for deciphering and reading the Aztec script. It is then divided into three historical chapters. This page includes a fifty-two year cyclical calendar, here framed in blue, with an eagle in the center. According to Aztec tradition, the gods sent this bird to land on a cactus tree, at the future site of Tenochtitlan.

merging them, or superimposing them. Thus, knowing each of these methods was required for a correct reading of the text. Once all these reading keys were taken into account, it was possible to decode the *Mendoza Codex* and learn for the first time some of the arguments discussed in the manuscripts of Moctezuma's subjects. This method was also applied successfully to other codices.

The seventy-two page *Mendoza Codex* is divided into three sections: the first section describes a historical period of 194 years, from the establishment of Tenochtitlan in 1325 to 1533, the year of the Spanish conquest. The second section is a list of taxes the vassal kingdoms were required to pay to the king of Tenochtitlan; the third section is an essay on the lifestyle and education of an Aztec warrior. This last section has yielded a wealth of information about interesting aspects of Aztec life, such as clothing and weapons. Similar data about the Maya world have come down to us only through painted pottery and wall paintings.

The officials wrote a number of explanatory notes at the end of the text when they sent it as a present to the king of Spain, proof that the book was meant to be simply a collection of illustrations without any written text. The first page of the codex illustrates a cyclical calendar lasting fifty-one years, beginning with the establishment of Tenochtitlan, and recounts the major events of the period.

Reading Key

The complex work of deciphering the codex is based on decomposing the elements that make up all the figures. This personage is one of nine dignitaries appearing on the first page of the Mendoza Codex. He is called Ocelopantzin, and this is how the reading key reads: "Venerable Ocelopantzin, jaguar-skin flag, great warrior, great noble of high nobility, he who sits, rules and judges."

PERU

Based on studies by scholars who looked into the possible existence of forms of writing in pre-Columbian Peru, several interesting theories have been set forth. One of the cultures that was reviewed for this purpose was that of the Moche, a people who flourished on the northern Peruvian coast between the second century B.C. and the seventh century A.D., almost one thousand years before the Inca.

The Peruvian archaeologist Raphael Larco Hoyle was the first to put forth the "bean writing" theory. He looked at a number of pictures on Moche pottery, which portray individuals, most likely messengers, wearing bird masks and carrying purses full of beans. Other scenes show divine beings looking at the same beans, and still others depict anthropomorphic beans.

These beans are unusual in that their surface is filled with at least twenty-two dots, parallel lines, diagonal lines, and filled-in spaces. Larco Hoyle found the same type of decoration on real beans discovered inside tombs. Thus, the archaeologist drew the conclusion that each bean was the "scroll" of an ideographic script, with the signs being punched on

Drawing of a recurring iconographic element in typical Moche ceramics: a bean with warrior-like features, armed with shield and spear.

the beans. According to this theory, the individuals portrayed on these vases were conveying "messages" written on beans. This theory is quite interesting, also on account of the frequency with which decorated beans were painted on vases. However, to date it has not been possible to prove it is truly a script, and no possible messages have yet been decoded.

Other scholars have put forth the theory that the beans were possibly used for gambling, similar to those the Araucanian Indians of Chile still use for the same purpose. If this were the case, the painted scenes would illustrate a sort of ritual game, possibly imbued with religious significance, where the beans served as dice or pawns. Many scholars are skeptical about these theories. Others believe that if indeed the beans were punched, if only for gambling purposes, this type of script would be ideographic. The field is open to all kinds of theories.

The specialist Hocquenguem has also researched the possibility that the Moche had developed a form of writing. According to her, almost all wall frescoes, vase paintings in particular, had a narrative purpose and could be considered as a type of "pictographic script."

Another rich and interesting field of research is the writing on textiles. Most pre-Inca Peruvian cultures, in particular the Moche and Nazca of the First Lower period, the Huari of the Middle Horizon, and the Chancay of the Second Intermediate period, have left evidence of a vast textile production, proof that these

Bean Writing

There is a long-standing debate among scholars of pre-Columbian civilization on the possible existence of a Moche writing that flourished many centuries before the Inca. It is a "bean writing" system, with dot-and-line signs written on a special type of legume, called pallares in Spanish. Beans with such decorations have been found among burial offerings and also appear in painted vases.

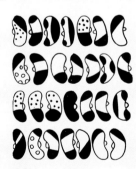

people had reached a high degree of technical and iconographic sophistication.

According to the work of Laura Laurencich Minelli, who recently studied the problem of ancient Peruvian writing, the many geometric designs, stylized naturalistic motifs, and complex scenes—similar to those painted on ceramic objects—are not simply aesthetic and casual, but contain some sort of written message to be interpreted by analyzing the images, the styles, and the colors of the textiles.

Other interesting theories have been put forth recently in the field of ancient Peruvian writing. According to Spanish chroniclers, the main tool the Inca used for writing was the quipu. In Quechua this word means "knot" and referred to a set of small, colored strings knotted on a main string, whose principal use was as a calculator and record book for accounting purposes: this was the numerical *quipu*. Spread out, the *quipu* looked like a wide fringe consisting of small strings laid out like the warp of a fabric: on each of these strings were the knots that corresponded to ones, tens, hundreds, etc., arranged from the farthest point inward in well-defined rows. The *quipu* was filed away by rolling it up. Thus the *quipu* could be defined as a sort of manuscript in

An anthropomorphic bean painted on a Moche ceramic. It represents a warrior armed with a club and a crescent-shaped knife typical of Peruvian cultures of the northern coastal area. According to some experts, the beans were used to write messages and were endowed with deep religious significance.

which the script consisted of strings and knots which could be simple or multiple. This type of script is called "string-writing."

Among the Inca, the Quipucamayoc were men in charge of reading these mnemonic devices, whose numerical key was interpreted by Loke in the first half of the twentieth century. A non-numerical reading of the *quipu* is still unclear. We do not know to what the numbers on the strings refer, based on the multiple combinations of the positions and colors of the knots.

Until recently, the general belief was that the *quipu* had a strictly numerical purpose, and was simply an accounting and computing tool that might have served, at most, for calendrical computations. However, the Miccinelli document from Naples has recently shown that at the end of the sixteenth and early seventeenth centuries literary *quipu* still existed on which were inserted textile ideograms, called key words, whose phonetic-syllabic reading composed a sacred text. This allows us to infer that the existence of this type of *quipu* might go back to the Inca colonial period.

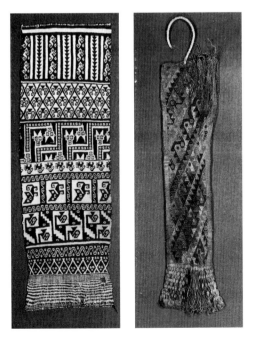

Elegant cotton textiles from the Peruvian central coast, with geometric and zoomorphic patterns that might be a type of writing on fabric. Biella, Alvigini Collection.

Additionally, the Miccinelli document points to the existence of another type of writing, this one ideographic, which consisted in repeating decorative geometric motifs by changing the color combinations on fabrics, jewels, and accessories. It does seem possible that in the near future scholars will be able to decode several types of scripts that were possibly used by the populations of ancient Peru. Although still in the early research stages, the field looks promising.

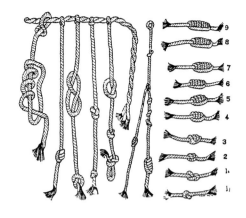

The quipu *was a tool used by the Inca to compose accounting and computational messages. According to recent research on the subject, there were also historical and literary quipu.*

As far as Mesoamerica is concerned, collaborative efforts by archaeologists, historians, and epigraphers have determined that different forms of script did exist, although they are very different from the Western forms of thinking and writing.

There is an intriguing mystery in the Ingenio Pampa, a vast desert area along the southern coast of Peru. A large number of geometric, especially zoomorphic, symbols were found engraved in sand by removing the surface layer of pebbles. Some scholars believe they compose an immense astronomical map; others

suggest that they might be calendrical symbols. What is certain is that many of the animals—such as the monkey and the hummingbird—drawn by these glyphs have specific meanings in South American religion and mythology. Because of their enormous size, these signs, also known as "geoglyphs," can be seen in their entirety only from a very high altitude such as from an airplane. The meaning and size of these geoglyphs is still a mystery. According to some scholars, they were created to be seen and contemplated only by the gods.

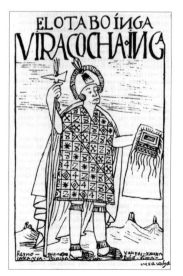

Far left: *The Inca Viracocha with a* tocapu *decorated with many symbols.* **Left:** *One of the Inca's secretaries with a* quipu. *From* Guaman Poma de Ayala, *figs. 106 and 358.*

THE WORLD'S GRAPHIC SYSTEMS

In concluding this study of ancient Maya script, we would like to briefly review the various graphic systems used in antiquity, or still in use today, paying particular attention to the meaning of the definitions that were attributed to such systems.

We may approach graphic systems, in the first place, by looking at the one we are most familiar with: the alphabetical system. This is the most common writing system in the West. No matter which language uses it, only a limited a number of signs is required, each of these signs corresponding to the phonetic value of a vowel or a consonant letter. For example, the English and French alphabet consist of twenty-six signs, the Italian of twenty-one, and the Russian alphabet of thirty-two.

Beginning in 1200 B.C., Phoenicians merchants and navigators spread the use of their alphabet throughout the Mediterranean: the first to adopt it were the ancient Greeks. Subsequently, the Arabs and Hebrews also adopted this system of writing.

Other systems also exist, more complex and more distant from our cultural world. One of these is the syllabic system, which in any case uses a much larger number of signs than the alphabet, between sixty and one hundred. To each sign corresponds a vowel or a consonant plus a vowel, i.e., a syllable. One important example of ancient syllabic script is the "Linear B," used by the Mycenaeans (1550–1100 B.C.), deciphered by J. Chadwick and Michael Ventris.

The Maya language from the Clas-

The text of the famous Phaeston Disc reproduced here has yet to be decoded, as it is written in an unknown language and writing system, foreign to the Cretan-Mycenaaean world. Eraklion, Archaeological Museum.

sic period as well could be expressed by a syllabic-type script.

Finally, there are ideographic, logographic, and pictographic systems. These are the three most ancient types of writings, very similar to each other, and we may consider them simultaneously. In all three systems, the signs are stylized figures that express a word, an idea, or a concept. For example, as we already noted, the Maya could write the word "jaguar" by using an image of the animal's head. Other writings that use these systems are those of ancient Egypt and China. An ideographic writing can have several hundred or even a thousand signs, which are required to represent the whole variety of language expressions.

Based on the research done on these texts, scholars have attempted to decode the writing of the Minoic Cretans known as "Linear A," so far without any success, for it is an unknown graphic system used to express a language that was neither Greek nor Indo-European.

Etruscan writing also continues to be a partial mystery. As we can seen from the jug on the left, it uses symbols derived from the Greek alphabet, applied to a non-Indo-European language.

FURTHER READING

In addition to my own still-unpublished research, I have consulted several texts on different aspects of Maya civilization to complete this book. Anyone wishing to expand his or her knowledge of the subjects reviewed here might want to consider the following bibliography.

Maya script, its decoding and historical evolution:
Coe, Michael D. *Breaking the Maya Code.* London: Thames and Hudson, 1992.
Fash, William L. *Scribes, Warriors, and Kings: The City of Copán and the Ancient Maya.* London: Thames and Hudson, 1991.
Harris, John F. and Stephen K. Stearns. *Understanding Maya Inscriptions: A Hieroglyphic Handbook.* Philadelphia: University of Pennsylvania Museum of Archaeology and Anthropology, 1992.
Houston, Stephen D. *Maya Glyphs.* London: British Museum Publications, 1996.
Schele, Linda and David Freidel. *A Forest of Kings: The Untold Story of the Ancient Maya.* New York: William Morrow & Company, 1990.
Schele, Linda and Mary E. Miller. *The Blood of Kings: Dynasty and Rituals in Maya Art.* New York: George Braziller, Inc., in association with the Kimbell Art Museum, Forth Worth, Tex., 1986.

Maya civilization:
Baudez, Claude F. and Sidney Picasso. *Maya. Alla scoperta delle città perdute* (Discovering Lost Cities). Milan, 1993.
Coe, Michael D., Dean Snow, and Elizabeth Benson. *Atlante dell'Antica America.* Novara, 1987.
Morley, Sylvanus G. and George W. Brainerd, revised by Robert Sharer. *I Maya.* Rome, 1984.
Thompson John E. *La Civiltà Maya.* Turin, 1994.

Maya art and architecture:
Baudez, Caude F. and Pierre Becquelin. *I Maya.* Milan, 1985.
Gendrop, Paul and Doris Heyden. *Architettura mesoamericana.* Milan: Electa, 1980.
Miller, Mary E. *The Art of Mesoamerica: From Olmec to Aztec.* New York: Thames and Hudson, 1986.
Olmedo, Vera B. *Le città degli dei* (Cities of the gods). Milan: 1992.

Maya religion and rituals:
Alcina Franch, José. *Miti e letterature precolombiane—Maya* (Pre-Columbian literature and myth—the Maya). Turin, 1992.
Leyenaar, Ted J. and Lee A. Parson L. *Ulama: Net balspel bij de Maya's en Azteken, 2000 v. Chr.—2000 n. Chr.: van mensenoffer tot sport* (The ballgame of the Mayas and Aztecs, 2000 B.C.–A.D. 2000: from human sacrifice to sport). Leiden: Spruyt, Van Mantgem & De Does, 1988.
Miller, Mary E. and Karl Taube. *The Gods and Symbols of Ancient Mexico and the Maya: An Illustrated Dictionary of Mesoamerican Religion.* London: Thames and Hudson, 1992.
Tentori, T. (editor). *Popol Vuh. Il libro sacro dei Quiché* (*Popol Vuh.* The Quiché sacred book). Milan, 1988.
Thompson, John E. *Maya History and Religion.* Norman, Oklahoma: University of Oklahoma Press, 1970.

We also recommend the following recently published works:
Stierlin, H. The Maya. *Palaces and Pyramids in the Rainforest.* Cologne, 1997.
I Maya di Copán—L'Atene del Centroamerica (Copán's Maya—The Central American Athens). Milan, 1998.

INDEX